Culturally Responsive Motivational Interviewing

Evidence-Based Adaptations for Latino/Hispanic, African American, Asian, Indigenous, Middle Eastern, and LGBTQ+ Communities

Travis Humphrey Shepherd

ISBN: 978-1-7642720-7-0

Table of Contents

Section I: Cultural Foundations

Chapter 1: Collectivist Adaptations for MI

The moment you walk into a therapy room with someone from a collectivist culture, traditional Motivational Interviewing hits its first major roadblock. The entire framework assumes something that might not be true: that your client sees themselves as an individual decision-maker who can and should chart their own course.

This assumption runs so deep in MI that we rarely question it. We talk about *personal autonomy, individual choice*, and *self-determination* as if these concepts translate seamlessly across all cultures. They don't. And when we miss this fundamental difference, we risk creating therapeutic relationships that feel foreign, uncomfortable, or even offensive to our clients.

Think about it this way: if someone's entire worldview centers on family harmony, community consensus, and collective well-being, how does it feel when a therapist keeps asking them what *they* want to do? What happens when we push for individual accountability in a culture where decisions flow through extended family networks?

The answer isn't to abandon MI altogether. The spirit of MI—that collaborative, respectful approach to change—translates beautifully across cultures. But the techniques? The language? The underlying assumptions about how people make decisions? Those need some serious rethinking.

Understanding the Individualistic DNA of Traditional MI

Let's start with the obvious stuff that's baked into standard MI training. Every core principle assumes Western individualism. *Expressing empathy* focuses on individual feelings. *Supporting self-efficacy* emphasizes personal capability. *Rolling with resistance* treats pushback as individual ambivalence rather than collective concern.

Even our reflective listening centers individual experience. We reflect back what the person said about *their* feelings, *their* concerns, *their* goals. We ask scaling questions about *their* confidence level. We explore *their* values and *their* reasons for change.

But here's where it gets tricky. In many cultures, separating individual experience from family or community context makes no sense. It's like asking someone to describe their left hand without mentioning it's connected to their arm. The connection is so fundamental that the question itself seems strange.

Consider this common MI approach: "What would you like to see change in your drinking?" Seems straightforward, right? But for someone from a collectivist culture, this question might feel incomplete or even selfish. Their internal response might be: "What I want doesn't matter as much as what's best for my family" or "I can't answer that without knowing what my community thinks."

Traditional MI also assumes that people can and should make autonomous decisions about their behavior. We build entire treatment plans around individual motivation, individual goals, individual commitment to change. The person sits across from us, and we work together to help them clarify their own desires and make their own choices.

But what if decision-making doesn't work that way in their culture? What if major life changes require family meetings, elder consultation, or community input? What if moving forward without that input would be seen as disrespectful or reckless?

This is where standard MI can accidentally become culturally insensitive. Not because we mean to be, but because we're operating from assumptions that don't match our client's reality.

The Cultural Collision in the Therapy Room

I remember working with Maria, a 45-year-old woman whose family had immigrated from Guatemala. She came to see me about her drinking, but every time I asked what she wanted to do differently, she looked uncomfortable. She'd give vague answers, change the subject, or talk about what her husband thought she should do.

Using standard MI techniques, I might have interpreted this as resistance or ambivalence. I might have reflected back her uncertainty or asked scaling questions to help her clarify her own motivation. But something felt off about that approach.

It took me several sessions to realize what was happening. In Maria's culture, making individual decisions about something that affected the whole family without consulting them first wasn't just unusual—it was wrong. My questions about what *she* wanted felt selfish and inappropriate to her.

When I shifted my approach to acknowledge her family context, everything changed. Instead of "What would you like to see change?" I asked, "How do you think your drinking affects your family?" Instead of focusing on her individual goals, we explored how her change might benefit everyone she cared about.

This doesn't mean Maria didn't have individual desires or that she couldn't make personal choices. It means those choices existed within a web of relationships that gave them meaning and validity. Ignoring that web made MI feel foreign and uncomfortable.

The same principle applies across many collectivist cultures. Whether we're talking about Latino families with strong *familismo* values, Asian cultures emphasizing group harmony, or African communities prioritizing collective well-being, the assumption of individual decision-making can miss the mark entirely.

Reframing the Spirit of MI for Collective Contexts

Here's the good news: the spirit of MI translates beautifully across cultures. The commitment to collaboration, the respect for client expertise, the belief that people have their own reasons for change—these principles work regardless of cultural background. But the way we express that spirit needs to shift.

Instead of focusing solely on individual autonomy, we can honor *relational autonomy*—the idea that people make their best decisions within the context of their important relationships. This doesn't mean family members make choices for our clients. It means our clients make choices with their family context in mind, and that's not only okay—it's healthy and appropriate.

Partnership in collectivist cultures might mean including family members in the conversation. It might mean understanding the client's role within their family system. It might mean respecting the decision-making processes that work in their culture, even if they don't match our Western expectations.

Acceptance becomes more complex when we're honoring both individual and collective values. We accept our client's ambivalence about change, but we also accept their need to consider family impact. We accept their pace of decision-making, which might involve consultation and consensus-building.

Compassion expands beyond individual suffering to include family and community impact. We feel for the person struggling with change, but we also understand the ripple effects throughout their support system.

Evocation shifts from drawing out individual motivation to exploring the intersection of personal desires and collective well-being. We help people find their own reasons for change, but we do it within the context of what matters to their community.

Adapting Core MI Techniques for Collectivist Cultures

Let's get practical. How do we actually modify MI techniques to work in collectivist contexts? It starts with changing our language and expanding our focus.

Reflective Listening can include family and community context. Instead of only reflecting individual statements, we can reflect the relational aspects of what people share. "You're worried about how your drinking affects your children" becomes "You're torn between wanting to relax after work and being the parent your children need."

Open-ended Questions can explore collective impact and decision-making processes. "How does your family typically make important decisions?" or "What would your grandmother say about this situation?" These questions honor the client's cultural context while still focusing on their experience.

Affirmations can recognize both individual strengths and cultural values. "You really care about your family's well-being" or "It's clear that being a good son is important to you." These affirmations connect personal motivation to cultural identity.

Summaries can weave together individual desires and collective considerations. "On one hand, you want to make this change for your own health. On the other hand, you're concerned about how your family will react. And you're trying to figure out how to honor both of those things."

The key is maintaining MI's collaborative spirit while acknowledging that collaboration might look different across cultures. Sometimes it means slowing down to honor relationship dynamics. Sometimes it means including family voices in the conversation. Sometimes it means recognizing that the client's "resistance" actually reflects healthy cultural values.

Language Adaptations That Honor Cultural Context

The words we use matter enormously when working across cultures. Small shifts in language can mean the difference between connection and disconnection, understanding and confusion.

Instead of asking "What do you want to do?" try "What feels right for you and your family?" This simple change acknowledges that individual desires exist within relationship contexts.

Rather than "What are your goals?" consider "What kind of person do you want to be for the people you care about?" This connects change to identity and relationships rather than individual achievement.

Instead of focusing on "your choice" or "your decision," we can talk about "finding a path that honors your values" or "discovering what feels authentic to you."

These aren't just semantic changes. They reflect a fundamentally different understanding of human motivation and decision-making. They honor the reality that many people find their strongest reasons for change in their connections to others.

Working with Extended Support Systems

One of the biggest shifts in collectivist MI involves expanding our definition of who's in the room. Even when family members aren't physically present, they're often psychologically present in our clients' decision-making process.

This means we need to understand family hierarchies, decision-making patterns, and communication styles. Who has influence in this family system? How are important decisions typically made? What would happen if our client made changes without family input?

Sometimes this means inviting family members into sessions. Sometimes it means helping our client navigate family conversations about change. Sometimes it means understanding why someone isn't ready to move forward until they've had certain discussions or received certain permissions.

I worked with David, a Korean American man in his thirties who wanted to address his gambling problem. Every time we got close to concrete action steps, he would backtrack or find reasons to delay. Traditional MI might have interpreted this as ambivalence or resistance.

But when I explored his family context, I learned that major decisions in his family required his father's input and approval. David wasn't ambivalent about change—he was trying to figure out how to approach his father about a shameful problem. Until he could navigate that family dynamic, individual motivation wasn't enough to move him forward.

We spent several sessions working on how to have that conversation with his father. Not because his father would make the decision for him, but because David needed his father's support to make the decision authentic and sustainable within his cultural context.

Case Study: Transforming Individual MI to Family-Centered Approach

Let me share a detailed example of how this plays out in practice. Rosa came to see me about her drinking, referred by her physician after some concerning lab results. She was a 38-year-old mother of three, married, with strong ties to her Mexican American community.

In our first session, I used standard MI approaches. I asked about her drinking patterns, explored her concerns, and tried to evoke motivation for change. Rosa was polite but seemed disconnected from the conversation. When I asked scaling questions about her readiness to change, she consistently gave low numbers.

Using traditional MI logic, I focused on exploring her ambivalence. I reflected her uncertainty and tried to roll with her resistance. But something felt forced about our interaction. Rosa seemed to be going through the motions without real engagement.

In our second session, I shifted approaches. Instead of focusing on Rosa's individual motivation, I asked about her family. How did her drinking affect her children? What did her husband think about her alcohol use? How would her mother react if she knew Rosa was concerned about her drinking?

Immediately, Rosa became more animated. She talked about wanting to be present for her children's activities. She shared concerns about being a good role model. She expressed worry about disappointing her mother, who had struggled with alcoholism years earlier.

But here's what was interesting: Rosa didn't see these family considerations as external pressure. She saw them as core parts of her identity. Being a good mother, a supportive wife, and a respectful daughter weren't obligations imposed on her—they were expressions of who she was and who she wanted to be.

When I reflected this back to her—"Being there for your family isn't just something you should do; it's part of what makes you feel like yourself"—she nodded enthusiastically. For the first time, she seemed to see the connection between change and her deepest values.

From there, our MI conversation took on a completely different quality. Instead of individual pros and cons, we explored how different choices aligned with or conflicted with her identity as a family member. Instead of personal goals, we discussed how she wanted to show up for the people she loved.

This didn't mean Rosa couldn't make individual choices or that her family controlled her decisions. It meant her individual choices gained meaning and motivation through their connection to her relationships and cultural identity.

By our fourth session, Rosa was making concrete plans for change. Not because she'd resolved individual ambivalence, but because she'd connected her desire for change to her cultural values and family roles. The change felt authentic and sustainable because it honored both her individual well-being and her collective identity.

Addressing Common Challenges in Collectivist MI

Working with collectivist clients presents unique challenges that require thoughtful navigation. One common issue is the apparent conflict between individual needs and family expectations. Clients might feel pulled between what they want for themselves and what their family expects of them.

In these situations, traditional MI might focus on helping clients assert their individual autonomy. But this approach can backfire in collectivist cultures, where family harmony is a core value. Instead, we can help clients find ways to honor both their individual needs and their family relationships.

Another challenge occurs when family members have conflicting opinions about the client's behavior or need for change. The spouse might want the client to quit drinking entirely, while parents minimize the problem. Extended family might offer contradictory advice.

Rather than helping the client choose sides, we can explore how to navigate these different perspectives respectfully. What does the client think each family member is trying to communicate? How can they honor the concern behind different opinions while making their own authentic choice?

Sometimes family members are actively opposed to change, especially if the client's problem behavior serves some function in the family system. The client might feel caught between their own desire for change and family pressure to maintain the status quo.

In these situations, we can help clients understand their family dynamics without becoming therapists to the whole family. We can explore how to make changes that don't unnecessarily threaten family stability while still moving toward health and well-being.

Building Cultural Curiosity into Your MI Practice

The most important skill for culturally adapted MI isn't technique—it's curiosity. Every client brings their own unique blend of cultural influences, family dynamics, and personal history. Our job is to understand their specific context rather than making assumptions based on ethnic background or cultural stereotypes.

This means asking questions about decision-making processes: "When you have important choices to make, how do you usually go about it?" It means exploring family roles: "What would your family say is most important for you to focus on right now?" It means understanding cultural values: "What does being a good [son/daughter/parent/spouse] mean in your family?"

These questions aren't intrusive if they come from genuine curiosity and respect. Most people appreciate when therapists take interest in their cultural context rather than ignoring it or making assumptions about it.

Building cultural curiosity also means examining our own cultural assumptions. What do we take for granted about decision-making, autonomy, and individual responsibility? How might our own cultural background influence our interpretation of client behavior?

When we can hold our own assumptions lightly while remaining genuinely curious about our clients' perspectives, MI becomes a truly collaborative exploration of change within cultural context.

Training Implications for Culturally Responsive MI

If you're a trainer or supervisor, these adaptations have important implications for how we teach MI. We need to move beyond one-size-fits-all approaches and help clinicians develop cultural flexibility within the MI framework.

This means teaching the spirit of MI as universal while acknowledging that techniques need cultural adaptation. It means helping clinicians recognize their own cultural assumptions and develop skills for working across difference.

Training programs should include opportunities to practice MI with clients from different cultural backgrounds. Role-plays should incorporate family dynamics and collective decision-making processes. Case discussions should explore how cultural context influences the expression and resolution of ambivalence.

We also need to address the challenge of working with interpreters, navigating extended family involvement, and understanding different communication styles. These aren't advanced skills—they're basic competencies for anyone working in diverse communities.

Most importantly, training should emphasize that cultural adaptation doesn't mean abandoning MI principles. It means applying those principles with greater flexibility and cultural awareness.

What This Means for Your Practice Moving Forward

As you think about implementing these ideas in your own practice, start small. You don't need to overhaul your entire approach overnight. Begin by paying attention to cultural cues in your current clients' language and behavior.

When clients talk about family opinions or community expectations, don't rush to refocus on individual choice. Instead, get curious about those relationships and how they influence the client's decision-making process.

When clients seem hesitant to commit to individual goals, explore whether family consultation or consensus-building might be part of their natural change process. Sometimes what looks like resistance is actually respect for appropriate cultural protocols.

Practice asking questions that honor both individual and collective perspectives. Notice how small changes in language can open up different kinds of conversations about change and motivation.

Most importantly, remember that cultural adaptation isn't about political correctness or walking on eggshells. It's about effectiveness. When we match our approach to our clients' cultural context, MI becomes more powerful, not less so.

The goal isn't to become an expert in every culture you might encounter. The goal is to become curious, flexible, and respectful of the different ways people understand themselves and make decisions about change.

When we can do that, MI retains all of its power while gaining the cultural authenticity that makes it truly accessible across diverse communities. That's not just good therapy—it's the kind of respectful, collaborative approach that MI was designed to be in the first place.

Moving Beyond One-Size-Fits-All Approaches

The future of MI lies in this kind of cultural flexibility. As our communities become more diverse and our understanding of culture becomes more sophisticated, we need therapeutic approaches that can adapt without losing their core integrity.

Collectivist adaptations of MI point toward a broader principle: effective therapy meets people where they are, not where we think they should be. When we honor our clients' cultural contexts, we don't compromise therapeutic effectiveness—we enhance it.

This doesn't mean abandoning everything we know about MI. It means applying what we know with greater cultural awareness and flexibility. The spirit remains the same; the expression adapts to fit the person and community we're serving.

That's what makes MI so powerful across cultures. It's not a rigid set of techniques—it's a way of being with people that can find authentic expression within any cultural context. When we remember that, we can serve our clients more effectively while honoring the diversity that makes our communities stronger.

Chapter 2: The Cultural Assessment

You can't use MI effectively with someone whose worldview you don't understand. This isn't about memorizing cultural facts or checking demographic boxes. It's about recognizing that every person who sits across from you brings a complex set of beliefs, values, and assumptions about how the world works—and these beliefs directly influence how they approach change.

Most clinicians skip this step. We jump straight into problem-focused conversations without understanding the cultural lens through which our clients interpret their experiences. We start exploring their motivation for change before we understand what change means in their world.

This is like trying to help someone navigate a city using a map from a different country. The streets might have similar names, but the layout is completely different. Without understanding their cultural geography, our best intentions can lead us both in the wrong direction.

The cultural assessment isn't a formal evaluation or a checklist of cultural characteristics. It's an ongoing process of understanding how culture shapes your client's relationship with problems, solutions, help-seeking, and change itself. It's about building a foundation of cultural understanding that makes every MI technique more effective and authentic.

Cultural Humility as Your Starting Point

Before we talk about assessment techniques, we need to address the foundation that makes cultural assessment possible: cultural humility. This isn't just being nice or politically correct. It's a fundamental stance that recognizes the limits of your own cultural knowledge and the expertise of your clients in their own cultural experience.

Cultural humility means approaching every client as an expert in their own culture, even when you think you know something about their ethnic background or community. A Mexican American client from Los Angeles might have a completely different cultural experience than a Mexican American client from rural Texas. Someone who immigrated as an adult brings different perspectives than someone who's third-generation American.

This humility also means recognizing your own cultural biases and assumptions. What do you take for granted about normal communication styles? What assumptions do you make about appropriate family relationships or individual decision-making? How does your own cultural background influence what you notice and what you miss in your clinical work?

I learned this lesson the hard way early in my career. I was working with Ahmed, a young man whose family had emigrated from Somalia. I thought I understood something about Somali culture from previous reading and training. I made assumptions about family hierarchy, religious influences, and community expectations.

But Ahmed's actual experience was much more complex. His family had lived in refugee camps for years before coming to America. His relationship with traditional Somali culture was complicated by trauma, displacement, and acculturation stress. His religious practice was influenced by both traditional beliefs and his experience in American mosques with different theological emphases.

When I finally stopped making assumptions and started asking questions, Ahmed became much more engaged in our work together. He appreciated that I was interested in his actual experience rather than what I thought I knew about his background.

Cultural humility isn't about pretending you know nothing. It's about holding your knowledge lightly while remaining curious about each person's unique cultural story.

Understanding Worldview Components in Assessment

Every cultural assessment needs to explore certain universal themes, even though the specific answers will vary dramatically across individuals and cultures. These themes form the foundation of how people understand problems, solutions, and change processes.

Relationship Orientation is perhaps the most crucial area to understand. Is this person primarily individual-focused, family-focused, or community-focused in their decision-making? How do they balance personal desires with relationship obligations? What does loyalty mean in their cultural context?

Some clients will approach change as an individual project. Others see change as something that affects the entire family system and requires family input. Still others might consider broader community impact or seek guidance from religious or cultural leaders.

Understanding relationship orientation helps you know who else might be involved in the change process, what kinds of resistance might emerge, and how to frame motivation in culturally authentic ways.

Communication Style profoundly influences how MI conversations unfold. Some cultures value direct, explicit communication. Others rely heavily on context, nonverbal cues, and indirect expression. Some emphasize emotional expression; others prioritize emotional regulation and control.

These differences affect everything from how people express ambivalence to how they indicate readiness for change. Someone from a culture that values indirect communication might express strong motivation through subtle cues that you could easily miss if you're expecting direct statements.

Authority and Hierarchy beliefs shape how clients relate to you as a professional and how they understand the change process itself. Some cultures emphasize egalitarian relationships and collaborative decision-making. Others have clear hierarchical structures with specific roles and expectations.

These beliefs influence whether clients expect you to provide direct advice or facilitate their own discovery. They affect how comfortable people feel disagreeing with you or expressing uncertainty. They determine whether seeking help is seen as strength or weakness.

Time Orientation varies dramatically across cultures and directly impacts how people approach change. Some cultures are future-focused and goal-oriented. Others emphasize present-moment awareness or honoring past traditions. Some see time as linear and controllable; others view it as cyclical and flowing.

These differences affect everything from appointment scheduling to goal-setting to understanding relapse as part of the change process.

Spiritual and Religious Frameworks provide meaning-making structures that can either support or complicate change efforts. Some clients integrate spiritual resources naturally into their coping strategies. Others experience conflict between religious teachings and behavioral changes they want to make.

Understanding these frameworks helps you identify spiritual resources and potential conflicts early in the process. It also helps you speak in language that resonates with the client's existing meaning-making systems.

Practical Assessment Strategies That Build Relationship

The key to effective cultural assessment is making it feel like natural conversation rather than formal evaluation. People are usually happy to share their cultural background when they sense genuine interest and respect. They become resistant when they feel like they're being categorized or stereotyped.

Broad Opening Questions work better than specific cultural inquiries. Instead of asking "What's your ethnic background?" try "Tell me a little about your family and where you come from." This invites storytelling and gives people control over what aspects of their background they want to share.

"How did your family end up in this area?" often leads to rich information about immigration history, economic circumstances, and cultural transitions that directly impact current functioning.

"What was it like growing up in your family?" opens up conversations about family dynamics, cultural values, and formative experiences without requiring people to speak for their entire ethnic group.

Curiosity About Decision-Making provides crucial information for adapting MI approaches. "When you have important decisions to make, how do you usually go about it?" reveals whether someone consults family, seeks spiritual guidance, does individual reflection, or follows some other cultural pattern.

"Who in your life gives you the best advice?" identifies key support people and cultural authorities who might influence the change process.

"What would your grandmother (or other respected elder) say about this situation?" often reveals cultural values and traditional wisdom that shape the person's perspective.

Exploration of Help-Seeking Patterns shows you how to position yourself and the therapeutic process in culturally appropriate ways. "What's it like for you to be talking to someone like me about this?" acknowledges potential cultural discomfort with professional help-seeking.

"Have you talked to anyone else about this concern?" reveals existing support systems and cultural resources that might complement or compete with professional intervention.

"What does it mean in your family/community when someone needs help with this kind of problem?" uncovers potential stigma, shame, or cultural explanations that influence engagement.

Understanding of Problems and Solutions reveals cultural frameworks for understanding difficulties and change processes. "How do people in your family usually understand problems like this?" shows you whether issues are seen as individual, family, spiritual, medical, or community concerns.

"What kinds of things have helped your family members with similar challenges?" identifies culturally syntonic interventions and resources.

"What would 'getting better' look like from your family's perspective?" ensures that treatment goals align with cultural values and expectations.

Recognizing Patterns Without Falling into Stereotypes

One of the trickiest aspects of cultural assessment is using cultural knowledge without making assumptions about individual clients. Cultural patterns exist and matter, but every person represents a unique combination of cultural influences, personal history, and individual preferences.

The goal is to use cultural information as a starting point for understanding, not as a predetermined conclusion. When you know that many Latino cultures value *personalismo* (warm personal relationships), you can pay attention to whether your specific client operates this way. But you don't assume they do just because of their ethnic background.

Similarly, understanding that many Asian cultures emphasize family honor and collective decision-making helps you notice these dynamics when they appear. But you remain open to clients who operate more individually or have complicated relationships with traditional cultural expectations.

Cultural Code-Switching is common, especially among people who navigate between different cultural contexts regularly. Someone might operate with traditional cultural values at home while adopting more individualistic approaches at work or school. They might feel comfortable with direct communication with you while preferring indirect styles with family members.

These variations aren't inconsistencies—they're sophisticated adaptations to complex cultural environments. Part of cultural assessment involves understanding how people navigate different cultural expectations and where they feel most authentic.

Acculturation Stress affects how people relate to both traditional and mainstream cultural values. Recent immigrants might feel pressure to abandon traditional approaches while simultaneously feeling disconnected from mainstream culture. Second or third-generation Americans might feel caught between family expectations and peer influences.

Understanding these dynamics helps you avoid pushing clients toward cultural choices that increase their stress. It also helps you identify the cultural resources and conflicts that influence their change process.

Working with Cultural Conflicts and Transitions

Many clients experience internal conflicts between different cultural values or expectations. Someone might value both individual achievement and family loyalty, even when these values seem to pull in different directions. They might appreciate traditional gender roles while also wanting more personal freedom.

These conflicts aren't problems to be solved—they're complex realities to be understood and respected. Your role isn't to help clients choose sides in cultural conflicts but to help them find authentic ways to honor their multiple cultural influences.

Bicultural Competence involves helping people develop skills for navigating different cultural contexts successfully. This might mean helping someone understand how to make individual decisions while still showing respect for family input. It might involve finding ways to pursue personal goals while maintaining cultural connections.

Cultural Flexibility becomes a therapeutic goal in itself. Rather than forcing clients to choose between cultural alternatives, you can help them develop comfort with complexity and context-dependent decision-making.

I worked with Priya, a young Indian American woman who felt torn between her family's expectations for an arranged marriage and her own desire for romantic autonomy. Rather than framing this as a choice between traditional and modern values, we explored how she might honor both her family relationships and her personal autonomy.

This involved understanding her specific family dynamics, her own relationship with Indian culture, and her vision for integrating different cultural influences in her life. The solution wasn't choosing one culture over another—it was finding her own authentic way to be Indian American in her particular circumstances.

Assessment as an Ongoing Process

Cultural assessment isn't something you complete in the first session and then forget about. Culture influences every aspect of the therapeutic process, and your understanding of your client's cultural context should deepen throughout your work together.

As trust builds, clients often share more complex or personal aspects of their cultural experience. They might reveal family conflicts, religious doubts, or cultural shame that they weren't comfortable discussing initially. They might help you understand subtle cultural dynamics that weren't apparent early in the relationship.

Your own cultural understanding should also evolve. Working with diverse clients teaches you about cultural patterns you hadn't noticed before. It challenges assumptions you didn't know you held. It expands your appreciation for the complexity of cultural identity in modern, multicultural contexts.

Cultural Check-ins can be built into ongoing sessions. "How is your family responding to the changes you're making?" keeps family dynamics in focus. "What would your church community think about this approach?" maintains awareness of religious influences.

"As we've been working together, have I missed anything important about your background or values?" invites ongoing cultural education and correction.

Case Study: Deep Cultural Assessment in Action

Let me walk you through a detailed example of how this process unfolds in practice. Carlos came to see me for help with anxiety that was affecting his work performance. He was 28 years old, described himself as Mexican American, and had been referred by his employee assistance program.

In traditional approaches, I might have jumped straight into anxiety symptoms and coping strategies. Instead, I started with broad cultural exploration.

When I asked about his family background, Carlos shared that his parents had immigrated from a small town in Michoacán when he was five years old. His father worked construction; his mother cleaned houses. Carlos was the first in his family to attend college and was now working as an accountant at a mid-sized firm.

This basic information already suggested several cultural dynamics that might influence our work: possible immigration-related stress, first-generation college experience, economic mobility, and potential conflicts between traditional and professional expectations.

When I explored decision-making patterns, Carlos described a family system where his father made major decisions after consulting with his wife and extended family. Important choices were discussed extensively before anyone moved forward. Carlos felt caught between this collaborative family style and the individual decision-making expected in his professional environment.

His anxiety, it turned out, was closely connected to cultural conflicts. At work, he was expected to be assertive, self-promoting, and individually competitive. These behaviors felt uncomfortable and inauthentic given his family's values of modesty, cooperation, and group loyalty.

Carlos also revealed that seeking professional help felt somewhat shameful in his family's cultural context. Problems were supposed to be handled within the family system, possibly with input from church leaders. Coming to therapy suggested that the family support system had failed somehow.

Understanding these cultural dynamics completely changed our approach. Instead of focusing solely on anxiety management techniques, we explored how Carlos might maintain cultural authenticity while succeeding in his professional environment. We discussed ways to manage family concerns about therapy while still getting the help he needed.

We also worked on *bicultural competence*—helping Carlos develop comfort with different cultural modes depending on context. He could be modest and collaborative at family gatherings while being appropriately assertive in business meetings. These weren't contradictory behaviors—they were sophisticated cultural adaptations.

The anxiety symptoms improved dramatically once Carlos felt he had permission to navigate different cultural contexts authentically rather than choosing one cultural identity over another.

Building Cultural Curiosity as a Clinical Skill

The most important outcome of cultural assessment is developing genuine curiosity about your clients' cultural worlds. This curiosity becomes a clinical tool that enhances every intervention you use.

When you're genuinely curious about someone's cultural background, they feel seen and understood in ways that go beyond symptom management. They become more willing to share difficult material, more engaged in the change process, and more likely to bring their cultural resources into therapy.

Cultural curiosity also protects you from making assumptions that could damage the therapeutic relationship. When you approach each client as a unique individual with their own cultural story, you're less likely to rely on stereotypes or generalizations that miss important individual differences.

Questions that Build Curiosity can be integrated naturally into any therapeutic conversation. "Help me understand what that means in your family" shows respect for cultural differences. "What would someone from your background think about that?" acknowledges cultural perspectives without making assumptions.

"How does your community typically handle situations like this?" reveals cultural resources and expectations. "What aspects of your cultural background are most important to you right now?" lets clients prioritize their own cultural identities.

Training Yourself to Notice Cultural Cues

Developing cultural assessment skills requires training your attention to notice cultural information that clients share, often indirectly. People reveal their cultural frameworks through the language they use, the concerns they express, and the solutions they consider.

Language Choices often reflect cultural values and assumptions. Someone who consistently talks about "we" instead of "I" might come from a collectivist background. Someone who mentions seeking guidance from elders or religious leaders is revealing cultural authority structures.

Pay attention to how people describe problems and solutions. Do they focus on individual factors or systemic issues? Do they emphasize emotional expression or behavioral control? Do they seek understanding or action?

Relationship References provide rich cultural information. How do clients describe family roles and expectations? What authority figures do they mention? How do they balance individual needs with relationship obligations?

Notice who they consult before making decisions and whose opinions matter most to them. These patterns reveal the cultural context within which change will need to occur.

Value Conflicts often emerge when people are navigating between different cultural expectations. Listen for tension between what they want personally and what their family expects, between traditional values and contemporary pressures, between cultural identity and assimilation demands.

These conflicts aren't therapeutic problems—they're normal aspects of multicultural living that require understanding and support rather than resolution.

Adapting Your Communication Style Based on Assessment

Once you understand someone's cultural background, you can adapt your communication style to match their cultural expectations while maintaining your therapeutic authenticity. This isn't about mimicking their communication patterns—it's about adjusting your approach to feel comfortable and respectful within their cultural framework.

Direct versus Indirect Communication styles require different therapeutic approaches. With clients who prefer direct communication, you can be straightforward about observations and suggestions. With those who prefer indirect styles, you might need to be more subtle, allowing them to draw their own conclusions from gentle questions and reflections.

Emotional Expression expectations vary dramatically across cultures. Some clients expect and appreciate emotional processing and expression. Others feel uncomfortable with emotional focus and prefer behavioral or cognitive approaches. Some see emotional control as a sign of maturity and strength.

Matching your approach to their comfort level doesn't mean avoiding emotions entirely with clients who prefer emotional regulation. It means respecting their cultural framework while gently expanding their emotional awareness in culturally appropriate ways.

Authority Relationships influence how clients relate to you as a professional. Some expect you to take a more directive, expert role. Others prefer collaborative, egalitarian relationships. Some want specific advice and guidance; others want facilitated self-discovery.

Understanding these expectations helps you find the right balance of expertise and collaboration for each individual client.

What This Assessment Process Achieves

When you invest time in genuine cultural assessment, several important things happen that enhance every other aspect of your therapeutic work.

Trust builds more quickly because clients feel understood and respected rather than judged or stereotyped. They sense that you're interested in their whole person rather than just their presenting problem.

Resistance decreases because your interventions feel culturally authentic rather than foreign or imposed. When therapeutic approaches align with cultural values, clients engage more readily.

Cultural resources become available for the change process. Every culture has strengths, wisdom traditions, and coping strategies that can support therapeutic goals. When you understand these resources, you can help clients access them.

Family and community support becomes possible because you understand the cultural context within which change needs to occur. Rather than working against cultural systems, you can work with them.

Therapeutic goals become more authentic because they reflect the client's actual values and priorities rather than your assumptions about what they should want to change.

Most importantly, **clients feel seen and valued** as whole people rather than collections of symptoms or problems. This feeling of being understood creates the foundation for all other therapeutic work.

Moving Forward with Cultural Assessment

As you begin integrating cultural assessment into your practice, remember that this is a skill that develops over time. You don't need to become a cultural expert overnight. You need to become culturally curious and humble.

Start by examining your own cultural assumptions and biases. What do you take for granted about normal communication, appropriate relationships, or healthy decision-making? How does your cultural background influence your therapeutic style and expectations?

Then begin asking more cultural questions in your current sessions. Notice how clients respond when you show genuine interest in their cultural background. Pay attention to how cultural information changes your understanding of their presenting concerns.

Most importantly, approach each client as an individual expert in their own cultural experience. Use cultural knowledge as a starting point for understanding, not as a predetermined conclusion about who they are or what they need.

When you can do that consistently, cultural assessment becomes a natural part of building therapeutic relationships that honor both individual uniqueness and cultural identity. That's the foundation that makes every MI technique more effective and every therapeutic outcome more sustainable.

Chapter 3: Addressing Systemic Barriers

The moment a client walks into your office, power dynamics are already in motion. You have professional credentials, institutional authority, and often cultural advantages that your client doesn't. These power differences can either support or undermine everything you're trying to accomplish with MI.

Most of us were trained to pretend these power differences don't exist or don't matter. We learned to focus on building rapport and therapeutic alliance without acknowledging the broader social context that shapes every clinical interaction. But ignoring power dynamics doesn't make them disappear—it just makes them invisible and therefore more likely to interfere with the work.

MI's emphasis on partnership becomes complicated when partnership isn't equally available to both people in the room. How do you create authentic collaboration when systemic barriers limit your client's choices? How do you maintain MI's spirit of empowerment when your client faces discrimination, poverty, or historical trauma that you've never experienced?

These aren't abstract theoretical questions. They play out in every session when you're working across lines of difference. The white therapist working with clients of color. The economically stable professional working with someone facing housing insecurity. The cisgender clinician working with transgender clients. The citizen working with undocumented immigrants.

Understanding and addressing these dynamics isn't about political correctness or walking on eggshells. It's about creating conditions where MI can actually work for everyone, not just for clients who share your social position.

Recognizing Power Dynamics in Cross-Cultural MI Encounters

Power operates in therapeutic relationships whether we acknowledge it or not. The question isn't whether power dynamics exist—it's whether we're conscious of them and how they influence our work.

Professional Power is the most obvious dynamic. You have training, credentials, and institutional authority. You can diagnose, recommend treatment, write reports that affect people's lives. In some settings, you might have legal authority to hospitalize someone or report to child protective services. This power exists regardless of your personal style or intentions.

Clients often come to you during vulnerable moments when they're struggling with problems they haven't been able to solve on their own. This vulnerability increases your relative power in the relationship. Even when you try to minimize power differences, the basic structure of professional helping creates inherent imbalance.

Cultural Power operates when you belong to dominant cultural groups that your client doesn't. If you're white and your client is a person of color, that cultural difference carries historical and contemporary power implications. If you're straight and your client is LGBTQ+, if you're cisgender and your client is transgender, if you're a citizen and your client is undocumented—all of these differences involve societal power dynamics that enter the therapy room.

These dynamics don't disappear just because you're well-intentioned or politically progressive. They don't vanish when you use collaborative language or try to minimize your expertise. They're woven into the fabric of how our society operates, and they influence how clients perceive you and your intentions.

Economic Power creates another layer of complexity. Most mental health professionals enjoy economic stability that many of our clients don't. We can afford health insurance, reliable transportation, and flexible schedules that make therapy attendance possible. We don't typically worry about missing work to attend appointments or choosing between therapy co-pays and other necessities.

When economic differences are significant, they can create invisible barriers to engagement. Clients might minimize their financial stress to avoid seeming irresponsible. They might agree to treatment recommendations they can't actually afford. They might feel judged for economic choices that seem irrational from a position of financial security.

Educational Power influences communication patterns and expectations in subtle ways. Most therapists have advanced degrees and are comfortable with abstract thinking, verbal processing, and psychological concepts. We assume certain levels of literacy and familiarity with educational systems.

Clients with different educational backgrounds might feel intimidated by psychological language or embarrassed about their communication skills. They might interpret educational differences as intelligence differences and feel inferior in the relationship.

Historical Trauma and Its Impact on Therapeutic Relationships

For many clients, current therapeutic relationships occur against the backdrop of historical trauma and ongoing systemic oppression. This history influences how they perceive professional helpers, what they expect from institutional relationships, and how much trust they're willing to extend.

Medical and Mental Health Betrayal has affected many communities in ways that directly impact current help-seeking behavior. The Tuskegee experiments, forced sterilizations, conversion therapy, pathologizing of cultural practices—these historical betrayals create reasonable suspicion about professional intentions and competence.

African American clients might approach therapy with warranted skepticism about whether white professionals can understand their experiences or provide culturally appropriate care. LGBTQ+ clients might question whether therapists will pathologize their identities or relationships. Indigenous clients might worry about cultural misunderstanding or appropriation.

This suspicion isn't paranoia or resistance—it's adaptive caution based on historical experience. Clients from marginalized communities have learned to protect themselves from professional helpers who claim to be helpful while actually causing harm.

Intergenerational Trauma affects families and communities across generations, creating complex relationships with authority figures and helping systems. Parents who experienced discrimination in schools might struggle to trust their children's teachers or counselors. Families with immigration trauma might avoid any contact with official systems, even helping systems.

Understanding these dynamics helps you contextualize client behavior that might otherwise seem resistant or uncooperative. When someone seems reluctant to engage fully in therapy, it might reflect protective strategies developed through generations of experience with hostile or incompetent systems.

Cultural Genocide and Assimilation Pressure have targeted many communities' traditional healing practices, languages, and cultural identities. Professional mental health has sometimes been complicit in these efforts, promoting Western individualistic values while pathologizing indigenous or communal approaches to healing.

Clients from communities that have experienced cultural suppression might approach therapy with concerns about whether engaging with professional helping means abandoning cultural identity or betraying cultural values.

Strategies for Building Authentic Partnership Across Difference

Acknowledging power dynamics and historical trauma isn't the end goal—it's the starting point for building authentic partnerships that can support meaningful change. The goal isn't to eliminate power differences (which is impossible) but to use your power responsibly and transparently.

Explicit Acknowledgment of power differences can paradoxically reduce their negative impact. When you name the obvious—that you have professional authority, that you come from different backgrounds, that systemic barriers affect your client's life in ways they don't affect yours—you create space for honest conversation about how these dynamics influence your work together.

This doesn't mean lengthy speeches about privilege or power. It means simple, direct acknowledgment: "I realize that as a white professional, I might not understand some aspects of your experience as a Black man in this community. Please let me know when I'm missing something important."

Or: "I know it can feel risky to be honest with someone who writes reports that affect your custody situation. How can we make this feel as safe as possible for you while still meeting the court's requirements?"

This kind of acknowledgment shows cultural awareness while inviting collaboration around managing the power dynamics constructively.

Transparency About Your Role and Limitations helps clients make informed decisions about how much trust to extend and what information to share. Being clear about confidentiality limits, reporting requirements, and institutional constraints reduces the chance that clients will feel betrayed when these realities become apparent.

"I want you to know that I'm required to report certain kinds of information, and I want to be upfront about what those are so you can make informed choices about what to share with me."

Or: "My training is in Western psychological approaches, so there might be cultural aspects of your experience that I don't immediately understand. I'm committed to learning, but I need your help to do that well."

Power Sharing involves finding genuine ways to shift decision-making authority toward clients, especially around treatment goals, pacing, and methods. This might mean letting clients set the agenda for sessions, asking for their input on treatment planning, or deferring to their cultural expertise about their own communities.

"What would be most helpful for us to focus on today?" puts the client in charge of session content. "What approach feels most comfortable to you?" acknowledges that there are multiple ways to address any given concern.

"You know your family and community better than I do. What do you think would work best in your specific situation?" explicitly recognizes client expertise while offering professional support.

Addressing Provider Bias and Assumptions

All mental health professionals carry cultural biases and assumptions, regardless of our training or intentions. The goal isn't to eliminate these biases (which is impossible) but to become aware of them so they don't unconsciously influence our clinical work.

Implicit Bias operates below conscious awareness and affects how we interpret client behavior, what we notice and ignore, and what interventions we suggest. Research consistently shows that even well-intentioned professionals make different clinical decisions based on client race, gender, sexual orientation, and social class.

These biases might lead us to pathologize cultural practices we don't understand, underestimate the impact of discrimination on mental health symptoms, or recommend interventions that don't account for cultural context and systemic barriers.

Addressing implicit bias requires ongoing self-reflection, consultation with colleagues from different backgrounds, and willingness to have our assumptions challenged by clients and communities we serve.

Assumption Checking can be built into routine clinical practice. Instead of assuming you understand what clients mean, ask for clarification. Instead of assuming certain interventions will work across cultural contexts, explore cultural fit before implementation.

"When you say your family is upset with you, help me understand what that looks like in your family" avoids assumptions about family dynamics while gathering specific information.

"This approach has been helpful for some people. What do you think about whether it would fit for someone in your situation?" acknowledges that interventions need to match individual and cultural contexts.

Cultural Consultation involves seeking input from colleagues, community members, or cultural consultants when you're working outside your cultural expertise. This might mean consulting with colleagues from similar backgrounds as your clients, attending cultural competency training specific to communities you serve, or developing relationships with cultural leaders who can help you understand community perspectives.

The key is approaching consultation with humility rather than defensiveness, viewing cultural learning as an ongoing professional responsibility rather than a one-time training requirement.

Case Study: Navigating Complex Power Dynamics

Let me share a detailed example of how these dynamics play out in practice. I was working with Keisha, a 25-year-old African American woman who had been mandated to therapy after a domestic violence incident. She came to the first session with obvious skepticism and minimal engagement.

The power dynamics were immediately complex. I was a white, male professional with institutional authority over her case. Keisha was facing criminal charges and potential loss of custody of her children. She had grown up in a community with complicated relationships with police and social services. Historical trauma, current legal vulnerability, and cultural differences all influenced our initial interactions.

Using standard MI approaches, I might have focused on building rapport and exploring her motivation for change. But ignoring the obvious power dynamics would have felt inauthentic and potentially harmful. Instead, I addressed them directly.

"I know this isn't exactly a voluntary situation for you, and I imagine it feels pretty frustrating to be required to talk to someone like me about personal things. I also realize that as a white guy working in a system that hasn't always been fair to Black women, you might have good reasons to be cautious about trusting me. How can we make this work for you while still meeting the court's requirements?"

This acknowledgment didn't magically eliminate the power differences, but it created space for honest conversation about how to navigate them. Keisha was initially surprised by my directness, then became more engaged as she realized I wasn't going to pretend these issues didn't exist.

Over several sessions, we developed strategies for working within the mandated treatment structure while still honoring her autonomy and cultural identity. We talked about how systemic racism had affected her experiences with police, courts, and social services. We explored how these experiences influenced her relationship with professional helpers, including me.

We also discussed the economic pressures that contributed to her staying in an abusive relationship—pressures that someone in my social position might not immediately understand. Rather than focusing solely on individual empowerment, we explored how systemic barriers limited her choices and what realistic safety planning looked like given her actual circumstances.

This approach didn't eliminate the power dynamics, but it made them workable rather than invisible. Keisha became more willing to engage authentically because she felt understood and respected rather than judged or stereotyped.

Working with Systemic Barriers Rather Than Around Them

Traditional MI often focuses on individual motivation and choice while minimizing attention to systemic barriers that limit those choices. But when clients face discrimination, poverty, immigration status concerns, or other structural barriers, individual motivation isn't enough to create sustainable change.

Realistic Goal Setting requires understanding the actual constraints within which clients operate. Someone facing housing discrimination might need different strategies for addressing substance use than someone with stable housing. Someone without legal status might need different approaches to family reunification than someone with citizenship.

This doesn't mean accepting systemic barriers as unchangeable, but it means working within current reality while potentially advocating for systemic change.

Resource Connection becomes crucial when individual motivation meets structural barriers. Clients might be highly motivated to change but lack access to resources that make change possible. Your role might involve helping them navigate systems, connecting them with community resources, or advocating for service accessibility.

Advocacy and Systems Change sometimes becomes necessary when systemic barriers prevent clients from accessing needed services or achieving therapeutic goals. This might involve writing letters to support immigration cases, advocating for reasonable accommodations, or working with community organizations to address service gaps.

The key is maintaining appropriate boundaries while acknowledging that individual therapy can't address all the factors that influence client well-being.

Building Cultural Responsiveness Into Your Practice

Creating culturally responsive MI practice requires ongoing attention to how power, privilege, and systemic barriers influence every aspect of your work. This isn't a one-time training or awareness-building exercise—it's an ongoing commitment to practicing differently.

Office Environment can communicate respect for diversity or reinforce dominant cultural norms. What artwork is displayed? What magazines are available? What languages are represented in signage and materials? These details send messages about who belongs and whose perspectives are valued.

Scheduling and Access considerations acknowledge that not all clients have the same flexibility or resources for attending appointments. Rigid scheduling policies might create barriers for clients with unpredictable work schedules, transportation challenges, or childcare limitations.

Payment and Insurance Policies can create or reduce economic barriers to care. Understanding how insurance systems work for different populations, offering sliding scale fees, or accepting community-based payment systems demonstrates commitment to accessibility.

Staff Training should include cultural humility, implicit bias awareness, and practical skills for working across cultural differences. Front desk staff, case managers, and other team members need these competencies as much as clinicians do.

Creating Psychologically Safe Spaces for Authentic Engagement

Psychological safety—the feeling that you can be honest without negative consequences—becomes more complex when power differences and cultural differences intersect. Clients from marginalized communities might need additional reassurance that authenticity won't result in judgment, discrimination, or harm.

Confidentiality Beyond Legal Requirements might mean being extra careful about how you discuss cases with colleagues, where you have conversations that might be overheard, and how you handle documentation when clients face additional vulnerabilities.

Flexibility in Treatment Approaches shows respect for cultural differences and individual preferences. Being willing to adapt standard interventions, incorporate cultural resources, or modify treatment goals based on client input demonstrates genuine partnership.

Patience with Trust Building acknowledges that clients from marginalized communities might need more time to assess your trustworthiness and cultural competence. Rushing intimacy or pushing for deeper disclosure before trust is established can backfire.

Response to Discrimination and Microaggressions becomes crucial when clients share experiences of bias or mistreatment. How you respond to these disclosures—whether you believe them, validate them, and take them seriously—significantly influences trust and engagement.

Training and Supervision Considerations

If you're a supervisor or trainer, addressing power and privilege requires systematic attention throughout professional development. These competencies can't be developed in single workshops or brief cultural competency trainings.

Case Consultation should routinely include discussion of cultural dynamics and power differences. Questions like "What cultural factors might be influencing this client's presentation?" and "How are our cultural differences affecting the therapeutic relationship?" should be standard parts of supervision.

Role Playing and Skill Practice should include scenarios that involve significant cultural differences and power dynamics. New clinicians need opportunities to practice addressing these issues explicitly rather than pretending they don't exist.

Personal Cultural Exploration helps clinicians understand their own cultural identity, biases, and privileges. This self-awareness becomes the foundation for working effectively across cultural differences.

Community Engagement provides opportunities for clinicians to learn about communities they serve outside the clinical context. Attending cultural events, participating in community meetings, or volunteering with community organizations builds cultural understanding and relationships.

What This Means for Your MI Practice

Integrating attention to power, privilege, and systemic barriers doesn't require abandoning MI principles—it requires applying them with greater cultural sophistication and social awareness. The spirit of MI remains the same; the implementation adapts to acknowledge social context.

Partnership becomes more complex but also more authentic when it acknowledges real power differences while working to minimize their negative impact. True partnership requires honest conversation about how social dynamics influence the therapeutic relationship.

Acceptance expands to include acceptance of systemic barriers and cultural differences that influence client choices and constraints. This doesn't mean accepting injustice as unchangeable, but it means working within current reality while potentially advocating for change.

Compassion deepens when it includes understanding of how systemic oppression and historical trauma influence current functioning. Individual symptoms often make more sense when understood within broader social context.

Evocation can draw out both individual motivation and cultural strengths, helping clients connect personal change goals with cultural values and community resources.

When you can integrate these principles with social awareness and cultural humility, MI becomes not just a therapeutic technique but a tool for social justice and cultural healing. That's not just good therapy—it's the kind of culturally responsive practice that our increasingly diverse communities deserve.

The Ongoing Journey of Cultural Responsiveness

Developing cultural responsiveness is a lifelong professional journey rather than a destination you reach. Every client teaches you something new about cultural dynamics, power relationships, and effective ways to work across difference.

The key is approaching this learning with curiosity rather than defensiveness, seeing cultural mistakes as opportunities for growth rather than personal failures. When you can hold your own limitations lightly while maintaining genuine commitment to cultural responsiveness, you create space for authentic partnerships that honor both individual uniqueness and cultural identity.

This work isn't easy, but it's necessary. As our communities become more diverse and our understanding of systemic oppression becomes more sophisticated, mental health professionals have both the opportunity and the responsibility to provide services that are accessible, culturally responsive, and socially just.

That's not just the right thing to do—it's the most effective way to help people create meaningful change in their lives while honoring the cultural contexts that give those lives meaning and purpose.

Section II: Community-Specific Adaptations

Chapter 4: Latino/Hispanic Communities

Personalismo and Family Involvement

When Elena walked into my office for the first time, she didn't just sit down and start talking about her drinking problem. She asked about my family, commented on the photos on my desk, and wanted to know how long I'd been working in the community. She shared stories about her neighborhood, her children's schools, and her job at the local hospital before we ever got to why she'd come to see me.

If I'd been using a standard MI approach, I might have gently redirected the conversation toward her presenting concerns. I might have interpreted her social conversation as avoidance or resistance. But Elena wasn't avoiding anything—she was doing exactly what felt natural and appropriate in her cultural context. She was building *personalismo*.

Personalismo isn't small talk or time-wasting. It's a fundamental cultural value that emphasizes warm, personal relationships over formal, task-focused interactions. In Latino and Hispanic cultures, you don't jump into serious conversations with strangers. You build personal connection first, establish trust through shared humanity, and create the relationship foundation that makes meaningful conversation possible.

When mental health professionals miss this cultural dynamic, we can accidentally create therapeutic relationships that feel cold, impersonal, or even disrespectful to Latino clients. We might interpret relationship-building as resistance when it's actually a prerequisite for authentic engagement.

Understanding and working with *personalismo* doesn't mean abandoning MI principles. It means applying them in ways that honor Latino cultural values while maintaining the collaborative spirit that makes MI effective across cultures.

The Role of Personalismo in Building Therapeutic Relationships

Personalismo reflects a worldview that prioritizes relationships over tasks, personal connection over professional efficiency. In cultures where this value is strong, people need to know you as a person before they can trust you with personal information or accept your professional help.

This means taking time to share appropriate personal information about yourself, showing interest in clients' families and communities, and approaching therapy as a relationship between two human beings rather than a professional service transaction.

Personal Disclosure becomes more important and appropriate when working with Latino clients who value *personalismo*. Sharing basic information about your own background, family, or connection to the community isn't unprofessional boundary violation—it's cultural responsiveness that facilitates therapeutic engagement.

When Elena asked about my family, I shared that I was married with two children and had lived in the area for several years. This wasn't therapeutic self-disclosure in the traditional sense—it was basic human connection that helped her feel comfortable with me as a person before we moved into professional helper roles.

Relationship Before Task means allowing time for connection-building even when it feels inefficient or tangential to the presenting problem. Latino clients often need to establish personal rapport before they feel comfortable discussing intimate concerns or accepting professional input.

This doesn't mean avoiding clinical work or spending entire sessions on social conversation. It means understanding that relationship-building is clinical work in Latino cultural contexts. The time spent establishing *personalismo* creates the foundation for everything else that follows.

Warmth and Authenticity become crucial therapeutic qualities. Latino clients often respond better to clinicians who express genuine warmth, use appropriate humor, and show authentic interest in their lives rather than maintaining professional distance or emotional neutrality.

This might mean hugging clients when culturally appropriate, sharing meals or coffee when possible, or expressing genuine emotion when clients share difficult experiences. These behaviors strengthen rather than compromise the therapeutic relationship when they align with client cultural expectations.

Understanding Family Decision-Making Processes

Familismo is another core Latino cultural value that emphasizes family loyalty, interdependence, and collective decision-making. Individual choices are viewed within the context of family impact, and major decisions often require family consultation or consensus.

This cultural value can create apparent conflicts with traditional MI approaches that emphasize individual autonomy and self-determination. How do you support individual motivation when the person sits within a family system that expects collective input on important decisions?

Extended Family Involvement often extends beyond nuclear family to include grandparents, aunts, uncles, godparents, and close family friends who hold *compadrazgo* relationships. These individuals might have significant influence over the client's decisions about behavior change.

Understanding who comprises the client's family system helps you identify potential sources of support or resistance to change. It also helps you understand the consultation processes that might need to occur before someone can commit to action steps.

I worked with Carlos, a 45-year-old man who wanted to address his gambling problem but kept hesitating when we got to concrete planning. When I explored his family context, I learned that he hadn't told his wife about the extent of his gambling losses. He was terrified of her reaction and couldn't imagine moving forward with change without her support.

Rather than focusing solely on Carlos's individual ambivalence, we spent time exploring how to have that conversation with his wife. We role-played different approaches, discussed cultural expectations about marital honesty, and planned for various possible responses. Once Carlos had that conversation and received his wife's support, his motivation for change became much clearer and more sustainable.

Collective Goals often carry more motivational power than individual goals for Latino clients with strong *familismo* values. "What kind of father do you want to be for your children?" might resonate more deeply than "What do you want for yourself?"

"How would your family benefit if you made this change?" connects individual behavior modification to collective well-being in ways that align with cultural values and increase intrinsic motivation.

Family Roles and Expectations influence how clients understand their responsibilities and possibilities for change. Traditional gender roles, birth order expectations, and generational responsibilities all shape what kinds of changes feel appropriate or possible.

These roles aren't necessarily rigid or oppressive, but they do provide cultural context for understanding resistance, motivation, and goal-setting. Working with these roles rather than against them often leads to more sustainable change.

Incorporating Religious and Spiritual Considerations

Religion and spirituality play central roles in many Latino families and communities. Catholic traditions, indigenous spiritual practices, and Protestant evangelical influences all contribute to Latino spiritual landscapes that directly influence attitudes toward problems, change, and help-seeking.

Catholic Influences might include concepts of suffering as spiritual growth, confession and forgiveness as change mechanisms, and community responsibility for supporting struggling members.

Understanding these concepts helps you work with rather than against existing spiritual frameworks.

Some Latino clients might view their problems as spiritual tests or consequences of moral failings. Rather than challenging these interpretations directly, you can explore how spiritual resources might support the change process.

"What would God want for you in this situation?" can be a powerful motivational interviewing question for religious clients. "How might your faith help you through this change process?" identifies spiritual resources that can support therapeutic goals.

Indigenous Spiritual Elements might include concepts of balance, connection to nature, ancestor wisdom, and healing through ceremony or ritual. These elements often coexist with Catholic beliefs in complex, syncretic spiritual systems.

Respecting these spiritual frameworks means taking them seriously as sources of wisdom and strength rather than viewing them as obstacles to rational problem-solving. Many Latino clients draw strength from traditional healing practices that can complement professional interventions.

Evangelical Protestant Influences have grown in Latino communities and might emphasize personal relationship with Jesus, biblical guidance for decision-making, and church community support for behavior change.

Understanding these influences helps you identify spiritual resources while also recognizing potential conflicts between religious teachings and certain therapeutic goals. Working collaboratively with religious leaders or incorporating biblical principles into change planning can strengthen rather than compromise therapeutic work.

Language Considerations Beyond Translation

Language shapes thought, and language choice reflects cultural identity and relationship dynamics. Even Latino clients who speak fluent English might prefer to discuss emotional topics in Spanish or use Spanish terms that don't translate directly into English.

Code-Switching between languages often reflects code-switching between cultural contexts. Clients might use Spanish when discussing family relationships or emotional experiences and English when discussing work or practical concerns.

Paying attention to these language patterns provides information about how clients categorize different aspects of their lives and where they feel most authentic or comfortable.

Emotional Expression varies between languages for many bilingual clients. Spanish might feel more natural for discussing feelings, relationships, or spiritual concerns, while English might feel more appropriate for practical problem-solving or professional communication.

When clients switch languages during sessions, it often indicates shifts in emotional intensity or cultural context. Rather than redirecting them to English, following their language choices can deepen therapeutic connection and understanding.

Cultural Concepts exist in Spanish that don't translate directly into English but carry important meaning for Latino clients. Terms like *respeto* (respect), *dignidad* (dignity), *vergüenza* (shame), and *orgullo* (pride) have cultural nuances that simple translation might miss.

Learning these concepts and using them appropriately in therapy shows cultural respect while accessing motivational frameworks that resonate with client worldviews.

Working with Interpreters becomes necessary when clients prefer or need Spanish-language services. Effective interpreter use requires understanding how to maintain MI spirit through translation, preparing interpreters for collaborative therapeutic approaches, and managing the three-way relationship effectively.

The interpreter should understand MI principles and be prepared to translate not just words but also the collaborative, respectful tone that makes MI effective. Pre-session briefings and post-session debriefings help ensure that therapeutic intentions translate accurately across languages.

Case Study: Family-Centered MI with a Latino Client

Maria came to see me about her drinking, referred by her primary care physician after concerning lab results. She was 38 years old, married with three teenage children, and worked as a school aide in a predominantly Latino district.

Our first session focused heavily on relationship-building. Maria asked about my background, shared stories about her neighborhood, and told me about her children's achievements and challenges. She talked about her job, her church, and her extended family before ever mentioning alcohol.

Using traditional MI, I might have gently redirected toward the presenting problem. Instead, I engaged fully with her relationship-building process, understanding that this was necessary foundation work rather than avoidance.

When we did begin discussing her drinking, Maria immediately framed it in family terms. She worried about being a good role model for her children. She was concerned about her husband's stress and how her drinking affected their marriage. She felt guilty about potentially disappointing her mother, who had strong opinions about women and alcohol.

Rather than focusing on Maria's individual relationship with alcohol, we explored how her drinking affected her ability to fulfill the family roles that were most important to her. We discussed what kind of mother, wife, and daughter she wanted to be and how alcohol use aligned or conflicted with those identities.

Maria's motivation became much clearer when we connected behavior change to cultural values and family relationships. She wasn't just quitting drinking—she was recommitting to the family roles that gave her life meaning and purpose.

But Maria also felt she couldn't make this change without her family's support and understanding. We spent several sessions planning how to talk to her husband and children about her concerns and her desire to change. We discussed how to include her mother in the process without triggering shame or judgment.

Once Maria had those family conversations and received support from her loved ones, her commitment to change became much stronger. The change felt authentic and sustainable because it honored both her individual health needs and her family relationships.

Six months later, Maria had significantly reduced her drinking and reported feeling more aligned with her values as a wife, mother, and daughter. The change process had strengthened rather than strained her family relationships because we had worked within rather than against her cultural values.

Adapting MI Techniques for Latino Cultural Contexts

Standard MI techniques can be modified to better align with Latino cultural values without losing their essential collaborative spirit. The key is understanding how *personalismo*, *familismo*, and spiritual frameworks influence therapeutic communication.

Reflective Listening can incorporate family and spiritual contexts. Instead of only reflecting individual emotions, you can reflect the relational aspects of client experiences. "You're worried about disappointing your family" acknowledges both individual concern and cultural context.

"It sounds like you're trying to balance what feels right for you personally with what feels right for your family" reflects the cultural tension that many Latino clients experience without suggesting they need to choose individual over collective values.

Open-Ended Questions can explore family dynamics and spiritual resources. "What would your grandmother say about this situation?" connects clients to cultural wisdom and family guidance. "How does your faith help you understand this problem?" identifies spiritual resources that might support change.

"What kind of example do you want to set for your children?" connects individual behavior to family roles and cultural transmission. These questions feel natural and meaningful within Latino cultural contexts.

Affirmations can recognize both individual strengths and cultural values. "You care deeply about your family's well-being" affirms cultural priorities while supporting therapeutic engagement. "Your faith is clearly a source of strength for you" acknowledges spiritual resources without requiring shared beliefs.

"It takes courage to seek help when your community might not understand" validates the cultural challenges of professional help-seeking while supporting the client's decision to engage in therapy.

Summaries can weave together individual desires, family considerations, and spiritual frameworks. "On one hand, you want to address this problem for your own health. On the other hand, you're concerned about how change might affect your family. And you're wondering how your faith can guide you through this process."

These summaries honor the complexity of Latino cultural decision-making while maintaining focus on change processes.

Working with Gender Roles and Expectations

Traditional Latino cultures often have clear expectations about appropriate gender roles and behaviors. These expectations can influence how men and women approach help-seeking, express problems, and consider behavior change options.

Machismo concepts might make it difficult for Latino men to acknowledge vulnerability, seek professional help, or express emotional distress. Understanding these cultural pressures helps you create therapeutic spaces where men can maintain cultural dignity while still engaging in change processes.

This might mean focusing on strength-based language, connecting change to family provider roles, or acknowledging the courage required to seek help despite cultural barriers.

Marianismo expectations might pressure Latina women to prioritize family needs over individual well-being, minimize personal problems, or avoid changes that might disrupt family harmony.

Working with these expectations means helping women find ways to care for themselves while still honoring family responsibilities. It might involve reframing self-care as family care or exploring how individual changes can benefit the entire family system.

Changing Gender Dynamics affect many Latino families as they adapt to different cultural contexts or generational changes. Second-generation Latino Americans might navigate between traditional family expectations and mainstream cultural influences.

Understanding these dynamics helps you avoid pushing clients toward cultural choices that increase family conflict while still supporting authentic personal development.

Community and Extended Family Resources

Latino communities often have rich informal support networks that can complement professional interventions. Understanding and working with these resources enhances rather than competes with MI approaches.

Compadrazgo relationships with godparents and close family friends create support networks that extend beyond blood relatives. These individuals might have significant influence over change processes and can become important allies in supporting client goals.

"Who are the people in your community who care most about your well-being?" helps identify these extended family relationships that might provide support or accountability for change efforts.

Church Communities often provide both spiritual resources and practical support for families facing challenges. Pastors, priests, and lay leaders might be willing to collaborate in supporting client change goals when approached respectfully.

Understanding the client's relationship with religious communities helps you identify potential resources while respecting appropriate boundaries between professional and pastoral care.

Cultural Celebrations and Traditions create opportunities for positive social connection and cultural reinforcement that can support behavior change goals. Understanding how clients want to participate in cultural events while maintaining change commitments prevents cultural isolation that might undermine therapeutic progress.

Addressing Acculturation Stress and Cultural Conflicts

Many Latino clients navigate complex relationships with both traditional cultural values and mainstream American expectations. This navigation can create stress that influences problem development and change processes.

First-Generation Immigrants might struggle with language barriers, economic pressures, and cultural isolation while trying to maintain traditional values in new cultural contexts.

Second and Third-Generation Americans might feel caught between family cultural expectations and peer influences, between traditional values and individual desires for autonomy or assimilation.

Understanding these pressures helps you normalize cultural conflicts while helping clients find authentic ways to honor multiple cultural influences. The goal isn't choosing one culture over another—it's developing bicultural competence that allows flexible navigation of different cultural contexts.

What This Means for Your Practice

Working effectively with Latino clients requires genuine respect for cultural values combined with clinical flexibility. This doesn't mean stereotyping or assuming that all Latino clients share identical cultural characteristics. It means being prepared to recognize and work with these cultural dynamics when they appear.

Relationship-Building becomes a clinical intervention rather than preliminary small talk. Investing time in *personalismo* creates the foundation for everything else that follows. Don't rush this process or interpret it as resistance.

Family Inclusion might be necessary for sustainable change with clients who value *familismo*. Be prepared to include family members in sessions, help clients navigate family conversations about change, or work within family decision-making processes.

Spiritual Resources can strengthen rather than compete with therapeutic interventions when approached respectfully. Learn about religious and spiritual frameworks that influence your Latino clients while maintaining appropriate professional boundaries.

Language Flexibility shows cultural respect and can deepen therapeutic connection. Even basic Spanish phrases or understanding of cultural concepts demonstrates commitment to cultural responsiveness.

Most importantly, approach each Latino client as an individual with their own unique relationship to cultural values. These cultural frameworks provide starting points for understanding, not predetermined conclusions about what any individual client needs or values.

When you can work skillfully within Latino cultural contexts while maintaining MI's collaborative spirit, you create therapeutic relationships that feel authentic, respectful, and effective. That's not just good cultural competence—it's good therapy that honors the whole person within their cultural community.

Chapter 5: African American Experiences

Addressing Historical Trauma and Mistrust

When James, a 35-year-old African American man, came to see me for depression, he spent the first twenty minutes of our session testing me. Not obviously or aggressively, but carefully and methodically. He asked about my training, my experience working with Black men, and my understanding of racism in mental health care. He shared a story about his uncle's terrible experience with a psychiatric hospital in the 1970s and watched my reaction closely.

James wasn't being difficult or resistant. He was being smart. He was doing what generations of African Americans have learned to do when dealing with predominantly white professional systems—he was assessing whether I could be trusted with his psychological safety.

This careful evaluation reflects the reality that African Americans have experienced centuries of medical and psychological abuse at the hands of professionals who claimed to be helping them. From the Tuskegee experiments to forced sterilizations, from pathologizing civil rights activism to misdiagnosing cultural differences as mental illness, the mental health field has a documented history of harming Black communities.

These experiences create what researchers call "healthy cultural paranoia"—a realistic wariness of professional helpers based on historical and contemporary experiences of discrimination and mistreatment (Grier & Cobbs, 1968). This isn't pathological suspicion; it's adaptive protection based on legitimate concerns about professional competence and cultural bias.

Understanding and working with this reality doesn't mean accepting permanent mistrust or therapeutic stalemate. It means recognizing that trust must be earned through consistent demonstration of cultural competence, respect, and genuine commitment to client welfare rather than assumed based on professional credentials or good intentions.

Understanding the Impact of Medical Racism on Help-Seeking

Medical racism isn't just historical legacy—it's ongoing reality that influences how African Americans experience and respond to professional helping systems. Research consistently shows that Black patients receive different treatment, face different assumptions, and encounter different barriers than white patients across all areas of healthcare.

Diagnostic Bias affects how Black clients' symptoms are interpreted and treated. Depression in African American men is more likely to be misdiagnosed as anger management problems or antisocial behavior. Trauma responses might be pathologized as personality disorders. Cultural strengths might be misinterpreted as pathological symptoms.

These diagnostic patterns reflect both implicit bias and cultural misunderstanding. When clinicians don't understand African American cultural expressions of distress, they might miss important symptoms or over-pathologize normal cultural responses.

Treatment Disparities persist even when diagnosis is accurate. Black clients are more likely to receive medication rather than therapy, more likely to be hospitalized involuntarily, and less likely to receive evidence-based treatments. They're also more likely to drop out of treatment, often citing poor therapeutic relationships and cultural misunderstanding.

Institutional Barriers create additional obstacles to accessing quality mental health care. These might include insurance limitations, geographic barriers, language and communication differences, and systemic discrimination within healthcare institutions.

Understanding these realities helps you contextualize client wariness and skepticism as rational responses to systemic problems rather than individual resistance or pathology.

The Legacy of Psychological Research and Practice

The field of psychology has its own specific history of pathologizing and mistreating African Americans that directly influences contemporary therapeutic relationships. This history isn't abstract academic knowledge—it's lived experience that affects how Black clients approach therapy.

Pathologizing Black Culture was standard practice in early psychological research and clinical work. African American family structures, communication styles, religious practices, and survival strategies were routinely labeled as pathological or dysfunctional rather than understood as adaptive responses to systemic oppression.

Even contemporary research sometimes continues these patterns by using white, middle-class norms as standards for mental health while treating cultural differences as deficits rather than variations.

Intelligence Testing Abuse used biased psychological instruments to justify educational and social discrimination against African Americans. The misuse of IQ testing to support racial hierarchies and limit opportunities created lasting suspicion about psychological evaluation and testing.

Civil Rights Era Pathologizing included attempts to diagnose civil rights activists and leaders as mentally ill, portraying justified anger about racial injustice as pathological rather than rational response to oppression.

These historical patterns help explain why some African American clients approach psychological evaluation and treatment with caution, even when current practitioners have no connection to past abuses.

Building Trust in the Context of Historical Betrayal

Trust-building with African American clients often requires explicit acknowledgment of historical trauma and contemporary realities rather than colorblind approaches that pretend race doesn't matter. This acknowledgment isn't about guilt or apology—it's about creating psychological safety through demonstrated awareness and cultural competence.

Historical Acknowledgment can be woven naturally into early therapeutic conversations. This doesn't mean lengthy speeches about slavery or civil rights history, but it does mean acknowledging the reality that African Americans have legitimate reasons to be cautious about professional helping relationships.

"I know that Black folks have had some really bad experiences with mental health professionals, and I want you to feel comfortable letting me know if anything I say or do doesn't feel right to you" opens space for honest communication about cultural dynamics.

Contemporary Awareness shows understanding that racism and discrimination are ongoing realities rather than historical artifacts. African American clients deal with microaggressions, systemic barriers, and overt discrimination that directly affect their mental health and daily functioning.

"Help me understand how racism and discrimination might be affecting what you're going through" validates these experiences while gathering important clinical information.

Cultural Competence Demonstration happens through actions rather than declarations. Clients assess your cultural knowledge through how you respond to their experiences, what assumptions you make about their lives, and how comfortable you seem discussing race and racism.

James, the client I mentioned earlier, was testing whether I would minimize his experiences of workplace discrimination, whether I understood the psychological impact of being the only Black professional in his office, and whether I could help him navigate cultural code-switching without pathologizing his adaptive strategies.

Incorporating Strength-Based Approaches Rooted in African American Culture

African American communities have developed remarkable strengths, resources, and survival strategies through centuries of adversity. These cultural strengths can become powerful therapeutic resources when they're recognized and incorporated rather than overlooked or pathologized.

Resilience and Survival Skills developed through historical and contemporary experiences of adversity represent sophisticated coping strategies rather than pathological adaptations. The ability to navigate multiple cultural contexts, code-switch between different communication styles, and maintain hope despite systemic barriers demonstrates remarkable psychological flexibility.

Rather than focusing solely on symptoms and deficits, strength-based approaches explore how clients have survived and thrived despite adversity. "How have you managed to keep going despite everything you've faced?" identifies existing coping resources that can support therapeutic goals.

Spiritual and Religious Resources play central roles in many African American communities and can provide powerful support for mental health recovery. The Black church tradition emphasizes community support, hope in the face of suffering, and collective action for social change.

"How does your faith help you get through difficult times?" explores spiritual resources without making assumptions about individual religious beliefs. "What role does your church community play in your support system?" identifies potential allies in the change process.

Family and Community Connections often extend beyond nuclear family to include chosen family, church family, and community networks that provide support, accountability, and cultural grounding.

Understanding these extended family systems helps you identify resources and navigate change processes that honor community relationships rather than emphasizing individual autonomy over collective support.

Cultural Pride and Identity can serve as protective factors and sources of motivation for change. Connection to African American history, culture, and contemporary achievements provides psychological resources for resilience and recovery.

"What aspects of your cultural identity are most important to you?" explores cultural strengths and values that can anchor therapeutic work. "How do you want to represent your community through the changes you make?" connects individual goals to cultural pride and responsibility.

Community and Church Involvement in Change Processes

African American communities often have rich informal support networks and cultural institutions that can complement professional mental health services. Understanding and working with these resources enhances rather than competes with therapeutic interventions.

The Black Church Tradition provides not just spiritual resources but also community support, leadership development, and collective action opportunities. Many African American clients find strength, meaning, and practical support through church involvement.

This doesn't mean all African American clients are religious or that churches are always supportive of mental health treatment. But for clients who do have positive church connections, these relationships can provide crucial support for therapeutic goals.

"How comfortable would you feel talking to your pastor about what you're going through?" explores potential spiritual support while respecting client autonomy about religious disclosure.

Community Organizations might include civil rights groups, professional associations, cultural organizations, or neighborhood groups that provide both practical support and cultural connection.

These organizations often have experience supporting community members through various challenges and might offer resources, advocacy, or peer support that complements therapeutic work.

Extended Family Networks frequently include not just blood relatives but also godparents, family friends, and community elders who play significant roles in decision-making and support provision.

Understanding these networks helps you identify potential allies in the change process while respecting family privacy and cultural boundaries around outside intervention.

Barbershops, Beauty Salons, and Community Gathering Places serve important social and emotional support functions in many African American communities. These spaces often provide informal counseling, community connection, and cultural grounding that support mental health and recovery.

Recognizing the therapeutic value of these community connections prevents the mistake of seeing professional therapy as the only valid form of mental health support.

Case Study: Working Through Historical Trauma and Mistrust

Let me share a detailed example of how these dynamics play out in practice. Marcus was a 28-year-old African American man who came to therapy following a depressive episode that had affected his work performance and relationship. He was successful in his career as an engineer but struggled with what he described as "imposter syndrome" and chronic stress.

Marcus entered therapy with polite but distant engagement. He answered questions appropriately but shared minimal personal information. He frequently qualified his statements with phrases like "I don't know if this makes sense" or "Maybe I'm overreacting."

Rather than interpreting this as resistance, I recognized it as reasonable caution from someone assessing whether I could be trusted with vulnerable information. Instead of pushing for deeper disclosure, I focused on demonstrating cultural awareness and clinical competence.

When Marcus mentioned stress at work, I asked specifically about being one of the few Black professionals in his company. When he described family pressure to succeed, I explored the cultural context of representing not just himself but his family and community in professional settings.

As Marcus realized I understood some of the unique pressures facing African American professionals, he began sharing more openly. He talked about the exhaustion of constantly managing racial dynamics at work, the hypervigilance required to avoid confirming negative stereotypes, and the isolation of having no colleagues who understood his experience.

Marcus also shared family history that influenced his current struggles. His grandfather had been denied educational opportunities due to segregation. His father had faced significant workplace discrimination despite his qualifications. Marcus carried both the pride of family progress and the pressure of not wanting to let previous generations' sacrifices go to waste.

We worked together to understand Marcus's "imposter syndrome" not as individual pathology but as a rational response to being in spaces where few people looked like him and where his competence was routinely questioned. We explored how to maintain professional effectiveness while preserving psychological well-being.

Marcus found strength in connecting his individual success to his family legacy and community representation. Rather than viewing his cultural identity as a burden, he began seeing it as a source of strength and motivation.

Six months later, Marcus reported significant improvement in his depression and work satisfaction. He had developed strategies for managing workplace racial dynamics while maintaining his authentic cultural identity. He had also connected with other Black professionals in his field and found mentorship opportunities within his community.

Addressing Internalized Racism and Cultural Shame

One of the most painful aspects of living with systemic racism is the way external messages about Black inferiority can become internalized, creating self-doubt, cultural shame, and psychological conflict.

Internalized Racism might manifest as negative assumptions about other African Americans, shame about cultural practices or expressions, or attempts to distance oneself from Black identity to achieve mainstream acceptance.

These patterns develop as protective strategies in racist environments but can create internal conflict and disconnection from cultural resources that support psychological well-being.

Cultural Code-Switching Stress affects many African Americans who navigate between different cultural contexts that require different communication styles, behaviors, and even personality presentations.

While code-switching can be an adaptive skill, the constant need to monitor and modify cultural expression can be psychologically exhausting and create feelings of inauthenticity or cultural betrayal.

Academic and Professional Achievement Conflicts might emerge when success in mainstream institutions seems to require abandoning cultural identity or community connections.

Some African Americans experience guilt about individual success when their communities continue to face systemic barriers. Others struggle with feeling caught between different worlds without fully belonging to either.

Working with these dynamics requires helping clients reclaim cultural pride while developing skills for navigating diverse contexts authentically rather than abandoning cultural identity for acceptance.

Adapting MI Techniques for African American Cultural Contexts

Standard MI techniques can be modified to better align with African American cultural values and communication styles while maintaining the collaborative spirit that makes MI effective across cultures.

Reflective Listening can incorporate cultural and historical context. Instead of only reflecting individual emotions, you can reflect the cultural and systemic influences on client experiences.

"It sounds like you're dealing with both the normal stress of your job and the extra pressure of representing Black professionals in your workplace" acknowledges both individual and cultural dynamics.

Open-Ended Questions can explore cultural resources and systemic influences. "How has your family history influenced your approach to this challenge?" connects current struggles to intergenerational strengths and resources.

"What would your grandmother say about how to handle this situation?" accesses cultural wisdom and family guidance that might support change processes.

Affirmations can recognize both individual strengths and cultural resilience. "It takes tremendous strength to keep going despite the discrimination you face" validates both individual effort and systemic reality.

"Your commitment to your family and community is really clear" affirms cultural values that can anchor therapeutic work and motivate change.

Summaries can weave together individual goals, cultural values, and systemic realities. "You want to take care of your mental health for yourself, but you're also thinking about how to be the kind of role model your community needs. And you're trying to figure out how to do both while dealing with workplace discrimination."

These summaries honor the complexity of African American experiences while maintaining focus on achievable change processes.

Working with African American Families

African American family structures are often more flexible and inclusive than nuclear family models, incorporating extended family, chosen family, and community relationships that provide support and guidance.

Extended Family Networks might include grandparents who played crucial parenting roles, aunts and uncles who provided financial or emotional support, and family friends who functioned as additional parents or mentors.

Understanding these networks helps you identify resources and navigate change processes that honor family relationships rather than emphasizing individual autonomy over collective support.

Intergenerational Trauma and Strength coexist within African American families, where stories of historical oppression exist alongside narratives of survival, resistance, and achievement.

Helping clients connect with family strengths while processing intergenerational trauma creates balanced perspectives that support both healing and empowerment.

Communication Styles might include storytelling traditions, call-and-response patterns, and emotionally expressive communication that differs from mainstream therapeutic expectations.

Adapting your communication style to match client preferences while maintaining therapeutic boundaries shows cultural responsiveness and facilitates deeper engagement.

Addressing Mental Health Stigma in African American Communities

Mental health stigma exists across all communities, but it takes on specific characteristics within African American contexts that are influenced by historical trauma, religious beliefs, and cultural survival strategies.

Strength and Survival Narratives emphasize resilience and self-reliance in ways that can make professional help-seeking seem like weakness or failure. "Black people are strong" becomes a cultural expectation that makes acknowledging vulnerability difficult.

Reframing therapy as building on existing strengths rather than fixing weaknesses can make mental health support feel more culturally consistent.

Religious and Spiritual Frameworks might view psychological distress as spiritual problems requiring prayer, faith, or religious intervention rather than professional treatment.

Working collaboratively with religious beliefs while offering professional support creates integrated approaches that honor both spiritual and psychological healing.

Community Protective Strategies might discourage sharing family problems with outsiders, especially white professionals, to protect the community from negative judgments or interventions.

Understanding these protective strategies helps you build trust while respecting appropriate cultural boundaries around family privacy and community loyalty.

What This Means for Your Practice

Working effectively with African American clients requires ongoing commitment to cultural learning, self-examination, and genuine respect for the historical and contemporary realities that influence therapeutic relationships.

Cultural Education becomes a professional responsibility rather than optional training. Understanding African American history, contemporary experiences of racism, and cultural strengths provides essential context for clinical work.

Self-Examination of your own racial identity, biases, and assumptions becomes crucial for developing authentic therapeutic relationships across racial differences. This work is uncomfortable but necessary for effective cross-racial therapy.

Trust-Building requires patience, consistency, and demonstrated cultural competence over time. Don't expect immediate trust or interpret initial caution as pathological resistance.

Strength-Based Approaches that recognize and build on African American cultural resources create more effective and culturally authentic therapeutic relationships than deficit-focused models.

Community Connection involves understanding and working with the informal support networks and cultural institutions that provide strength and resources for African American clients.

Most importantly, approach each African American client as an individual with their own unique relationship to cultural identity, community connection, and experiences of racism. Cultural knowledge provides important context, but individual assessment and respect for personal experience remain essential.

When you can work skillfully within these cultural contexts while maintaining MI's collaborative spirit, you create therapeutic relationships that honor both individual healing and cultural strength. That's not just culturally responsive therapy—it's effective therapy that supports both personal recovery and community resilience.

Chapter 6: Asian Cultures

Harmony, Hierarchy, and Indirect Communication

When Dr. Chen brought her 16-year-old son Kevin to see me for what she described as "attitude problems," the first thing I noticed was how they sat in my office. Dr. Chen took the lead in explaining the situation while Kevin sat quietly, making minimal eye contact and speaking only when directly addressed. When I asked Kevin about his perspective, he glanced at his mother before responding with brief, carefully neutral statements.

Using Western therapeutic approaches, I might have interpreted Kevin's behavior as resistance, family enmeshment, or lack of individual autonomy. I might have tried to engage him more directly or encouraged him to express his own opinions more forcefully. But that would have missed the cultural dynamics that were actually unfolding in my office.

Kevin wasn't being resistant or overly dependent. He was demonstrating appropriate respect for his mother's authority and showing consideration for family harmony by not openly contradicting her in front of an outsider. His indirect communication style reflected cultural values that prioritize group cohesion over individual expression.

Dr. Chen wasn't being controlling or overprotective. She was fulfilling her cultural role as family spokesperson and advocate while trying to preserve Kevin's dignity by handling the family's problems discretely rather than exposing him to potential shame or judgment.

Understanding these cultural dynamics completely changed how I approached our work together. Instead of pushing for individual expression and family differentiation, I worked within the cultural framework of respect, harmony, and appropriate hierarchy while still addressing the underlying concerns that brought them to therapy.

This experience taught me that effective MI with Asian clients requires understanding cultural values that can seem to conflict with Western therapeutic assumptions about healthy communication and family functioning. The key is adapting MI techniques to honor these cultural values while still facilitating meaningful change.

Navigating Concepts of Face and Shame in MI Conversations

The concept of "face" (*mianzi* in Chinese, *mentsu* in Japanese, *chaemyeon* in Korean) represents social dignity, reputation, and standing within the community. Maintaining face isn't vanity or superficiality—it's a complex social system that governs relationships, communication, and behavior in profound ways.

Saving Face involves protecting someone's dignity and reputation, especially in social situations where mistakes or problems might become visible to others. This protection extends to family members, whose behavior reflects on the entire family's reputation.

When Asian clients come to therapy, they're often already experiencing shame about needing outside help. The act of seeking professional assistance can feel like public admission of family failure or individual inadequacy.

Understanding this dynamic helps you create therapeutic environments that protect rather than threaten client dignity. This might mean being extra careful about confidentiality, avoiding questions that require admission of serious mistakes, or framing problems in ways that don't imply personal or family failure.

Losing Face happens when someone's dignity or competence is questioned publicly, when they're forced to admit mistakes in front of others, or when their problems become visible to their community.

Traditional MI approaches that encourage detailed exploration of problem behaviors or explicit admission of mistakes can inadvertently threaten face and create therapeutic resistance.

Instead of asking "What problems has your drinking caused in your life?" try "What concerns do you have about how alcohol might be affecting your goals?" This subtle shift explores the same territory while protecting dignity and avoiding explicit problem admission.

Giving Face involves showing respect for someone's status, acknowledging their competence, and treating them with appropriate dignity. This becomes crucial in therapeutic relationships where cultural differences in status and authority might create face-threatening dynamics.

Asian clients might need explicit recognition of their efforts, accomplishments, and cultural wisdom before they feel comfortable acknowledging areas where change might be beneficial.

Understanding Shame Versus Guilt Cultures

Western therapeutic approaches often assume "guilt culture" dynamics where people feel bad about specific actions they've taken. Asian cultures often operate more on "shame culture" principles where people feel bad about who they are or how they appear to others.

Guilt focuses on specific behaviors: "I did something wrong." This creates opportunities for behavior change, amends-making, and specific problem-solving that align well with traditional therapeutic approaches.

Shame focuses on identity and social standing: "I am fundamentally flawed" or "I have brought dishonor to my family." This creates more complex therapeutic challenges because the problem isn't just changing behavior—it's restoring social harmony and personal dignity.

When Asian clients express shame about their problems, traditional MI approaches that focus on individual motivation and behavior change might miss the deeper concerns about family honor, community standing, and social relationships.

Working with shame requires helping clients find ways to address problems while preserving dignity and restoring social harmony rather than just changing individual behavior.

Adapting Reflective Listening for Indirect Communication Styles

Many Asian cultures value indirect communication that preserves relationships and avoids confrontation. This communication style can seem evasive or unclear to Western therapists trained to value direct, explicit expression.

High-Context Communication relies heavily on nonverbal cues, shared cultural understanding, and indirect expression. The meaning isn't just in the words—it's in the context, tone, and cultural framework surrounding the communication.

When Asian clients make statements like "Maybe I should consider whether my current approach is working as well as it could," they might be expressing serious concerns about major problems while maintaining appropriate cultural restraint.

Effective reflective listening requires understanding these indirect expressions and reflecting back both the surface message and the deeper concerns without forcing premature directness.

Nonverbal Communication carries enormous weight in Asian cultures. Silence might indicate respect, consideration, or disagreement. Lack of eye contact might show appropriate deference rather than avoidance. Physical posture and facial expressions communicate information that words don't express.

Learning to read and respect these nonverbal patterns helps you understand what clients are communicating beyond their spoken words.

Circular Communication might explore topics indirectly, returning to important themes multiple times from different angles rather than addressing them head-on immediately.

This isn't avoidance or resistance—it's culturally appropriate way of approaching sensitive topics that allows for face-saving and relationship preservation while still addressing important concerns.

Case Study: Working Within Hierarchical Family Structures

Let me share a detailed example of how these dynamics played out in my work with the Kim family. Mrs. Kim came to see me about her 20-year-old daughter Sarah, who was struggling with anxiety and academic pressure at university.

The family structure was clearly hierarchical. Mrs. Kim made the initial appointment, explained the family's concerns, and expected to be involved in treatment planning. Mr. Kim, though less verbally active, clearly held significant authority in family decision-making. Sarah, despite being an adult, deferred to her parents' perspectives and seemed reluctant to express different opinions.

Using Western approaches, I might have focused on helping Sarah develop individual autonomy and direct communication with her parents. I might have interpreted the family hierarchy as pathological enmeshment that needed to be challenged.

Instead, I worked within the existing family structure while creating space for Sarah's individual needs to be addressed. I showed appropriate respect for Mr. and Mrs. Kim's parental authority while gradually creating opportunities for Sarah to express her own perspectives.

When discussing Sarah's anxiety, I framed it as a family concern rather than individual pathology. "The whole family is worried about Sarah's stress level" honored the collective nature of the problem while avoiding individual blame or shame.

I asked questions that explored Sarah's experiences while maintaining respect for family hierarchy: "Mrs. Kim, you know Sarah better than anyone. What changes have you noticed in her stress level?" This positioned Mrs. Kim as the expert while gathering information about Sarah's functioning.

Gradually, I was able to create space for Sarah to share her own perspective without directly challenging family authority. "Sarah, your mother is clearly very concerned about you. What would help her worry less?" allowed Sarah to express her needs while framing them as ways to help her mother rather than individual demands.

Over several sessions, we developed a treatment approach that addressed Sarah's anxiety while honoring family values and maintaining appropriate relationships. Sarah learned stress management techniques, but she also learned how to communicate about her needs in ways that showed respect for her parents' concerns.

The family found ways to support Sarah's academic success while reducing the pressure that was contributing to her anxiety. Most importantly, Sarah felt supported by her family rather than caught between individual therapy goals and cultural expectations.

Working with Academic and Achievement Pressure

Academic achievement often carries enormous cultural significance in Asian families, representing not just individual success but family honor, intergenerational sacrifice, and cultural identity.

Educational Investment reflects generations of family sacrifice and cultural values that prioritize learning, discipline, and advancement. Parents might have given up personal opportunities to invest in their children's education, creating intense pressure for academic success.

Cultural Identity becomes tied to academic achievement in ways that can make school problems feel like cultural betrayal or family failure. Students might feel they're not just letting themselves down but dishonoring their family and culture.

Future Security depends heavily on educational credentials in ways that can make academic struggles feel like threats to basic survival and family stability.

Understanding these dynamics helps you work with rather than against achievement pressure while addressing the anxiety and perfectionism that can interfere with actual learning and success.

Instead of challenging the importance of academic success, help families find sustainable approaches that honor educational values while preserving mental health and family relationships.

Religious and Philosophical Frameworks

Asian cultures encompass diverse religious and philosophical traditions—Buddhism, Taoism, Confucianism, Hinduism, Christianity, and others—that influence understanding of problems, change, and helping relationships.

Buddhist Influences might emphasize impermanence, suffering as part of life, meditation and mindfulness practices, and interconnectedness of all things. These concepts can provide resources for understanding and coping with problems while also influencing expectations about change processes.

Clients influenced by Buddhist thinking might approach problems with acceptance rather than urgency for change. They might see suffering as meaningful rather than something to be eliminated quickly.

Confucian Values emphasize respect for authority, education, family loyalty, and social harmony. These values influence family relationships, help-seeking behavior, and attitudes toward change in ways that can seem to conflict with Western therapeutic approaches.

Taoist Principles focus on balance, natural flow, and non-action (*wu wei*) that allows change to happen organically rather than through forced intervention. Clients with Taoist influences might prefer gradual, subtle changes over dramatic behavioral modifications.

Understanding these philosophical frameworks helps you work within rather than against existing meaning-making systems while offering professional support that complements rather than conflicts with spiritual resources.

Language and Translation Considerations

Language barriers create additional complexity when working with Asian clients who might speak English fluently in professional contexts but prefer to process emotions and family issues in their native language.

Emotional Expression often feels more natural and authentic in one's first language, especially when discussing family relationships, cultural conflicts, or spiritual concerns.

Allowing clients to use their native language when needed, even if you don't speak it, can facilitate deeper emotional processing. Working with cultural interpreters becomes necessary when language barriers interfere with therapeutic communication.

Cultural Concepts exist in Asian languages that don't translate directly into English but carry important psychological and relational meaning.

Terms like the Japanese concept of *amae* (interdependent intimacy), the Chinese idea of *guanxi* (relationship networks), or the Korean principle of *jeong* (deep emotional connection) represent cultural frameworks that influence how people understand relationships and problems.

Family Communication Patterns might include different languages for different relationships (speaking English with children but Korean with parents) or different levels of formality that reflect family hierarchy and respect patterns.

Understanding these language dynamics helps you work within rather than against existing family communication systems while facilitating therapeutic conversations.

Gender Roles and Expectations

Traditional Asian cultures often have specific expectations about appropriate gender roles and behaviors that influence how men and women express problems, seek help, and approach change.

Male Role Expectations might emphasize emotional control, family leadership, and stoic endurance of difficulties. These expectations can make it particularly challenging for Asian men to acknowledge vulnerability, express emotions, or seek professional help.

Working with Asian men might require alternative approaches that honor cultural expectations while still addressing underlying concerns. Framing therapy as education or skills development rather than emotional healing can make the process feel more culturally appropriate.

Female Role Expectations might emphasize family harmony, self-sacrifice, and indirect communication. Asian women might minimize their own needs, avoid expressing disagreement with family members, or feel conflicted about prioritizing individual well-being over collective family needs.

Understanding these role expectations helps you avoid pathologizing culturally appropriate behavior while still supporting individual growth and family health.

Intergenerational Gender Conflicts emerge when traditional gender expectations clash with contemporary opportunities and expectations, especially for younger Asian Americans navigating between cultural worlds.

Working with Intergenerational Cultural Conflicts

Many Asian American families navigate complex tensions between traditional cultural values and contemporary American expectations. These conflicts affect family relationships, individual identity development, and approaches to problem-solving.

First-Generation Immigrants might maintain strong connections to traditional cultural values while adapting to new cultural contexts. They often face pressure to preserve cultural identity while achieving success in mainstream American society.

Second and Later Generations might feel caught between family cultural expectations and peer influences, between traditional values and individual desires for autonomy or cultural integration.

These generational differences can create family conflicts that require culturally sensitive intervention rather than taking sides between traditional and contemporary values.

Cultural Code-Switching becomes a necessary survival skill for many Asian Americans who navigate between different cultural contexts that require different behaviors, communication styles, and even personality presentations.

Understanding and normalizing these cultural adaptations helps clients develop comfort with cultural flexibility rather than feeling like they must choose one cultural identity over another.

Adapting MI Techniques for Asian Cultural Contexts

Standard MI techniques can be modified to better align with Asian cultural values while maintaining the collaborative spirit that makes MI effective across cultures.

Reflective Listening can incorporate face-saving language and indirect communication patterns. Instead of reflecting problems directly, reflect concerns and considerations that maintain dignity while acknowledging difficulties.

"You're thinking carefully about what approach might work best for your family" reflects problem-solving efforts while avoiding explicit problem admission.

Open-Ended Questions can explore cultural values and family wisdom. "What would your grandparents say about handling this situation?" accesses cultural guidance while showing respect for traditional wisdom.

"How do you think about balancing individual needs with family harmony?" explores cultural tensions without suggesting that either individual or collective values are wrong.

Affirmations can recognize cultural strengths and values. "Your respect for your family is really clear" affirms cultural priorities while supporting therapeutic engagement.

"It takes wisdom to think carefully about all the people who might be affected by this decision" validates indirect decision-making processes rather than pushing for immediate individual choice.

Summaries can weave together individual concerns, family considerations, and cultural values without creating artificial choices between them.

"You want to address this concern for your own well-being, but you're also thinking about how any changes might affect your family relationships and your standing in the community. And you're trying to find an approach that honors both your individual needs and your cultural values."

Mental Health Stigma in Asian Communities

Mental health stigma takes specific forms within Asian communities that are influenced by cultural values around face, family honor, and approaches to problem-solving.

Individual Problems as Family Shame means that one person's mental health struggles can feel like reflection of family failure or inadequate parenting. This creates pressure to handle problems privately rather than seeking outside help.

Cultural Solutions First might include trying traditional healing approaches, consulting with religious or community leaders, or attempting to resolve problems through family support before considering professional intervention.

Respecting these cultural approaches while offering professional support creates integrated healing approaches rather than competing with existing cultural resources.

Community Reputation Concerns influence willingness to seek help, especially from professionals who might not maintain appropriate cultural confidentiality or who might not understand the importance of protecting family dignity.

What This Means for Your Practice

Working effectively with Asian clients requires genuine respect for cultural values that might seem to conflict with Western therapeutic assumptions about healthy communication and individual autonomy.

Patience with Indirect Communication becomes a clinical skill rather than therapeutic obstacle. Allow time for circular communication patterns, learn to read nonverbal cues, and resist pushing for premature directness.

Respect for Hierarchy doesn't mean accepting unhealthy family dynamics, but it does mean working within existing family structures while creating space for individual needs to be addressed appropriately.

Face-Saving Approaches protect client dignity while still addressing problem areas. Frame difficulties as concerns rather than failures, focus on growth rather than deficits, and avoid therapeutic approaches that require public admission of serious mistakes.

Cultural Resource Integration involves understanding and working with religious, philosophical, and traditional healing approaches rather than viewing them as obstacles to professional treatment.

Most importantly, approach each Asian client as an individual with their own unique relationship to cultural values and traditions. Cultural knowledge provides important context, but individual assessment and respect for personal experience remain essential.

When you can work skillfully within these cultural contexts while maintaining MI's collaborative spirit, you create therapeutic relationships that honor both individual healing and cultural values. That's culturally responsive therapy that supports both personal growth and cultural authenticity.

Chapter 7: Integrating Traditional Healing with MI

When Mary Crow Feather first came to see me, she didn't come alone. She brought her grandmother's teachings, her tribe's understanding of healing, and generations of wisdom about how people find their way back to wellness. She also brought deep suspicion about whether a non-Native therapist could possibly understand her experience or provide culturally appropriate help.

Mary had struggled with alcohol use for several years, but she'd tried treatment programs before and felt like they missed something essential about her identity and healing process. The previous programs focused on individual pathology and behavioral change without acknowledging her cultural identity, spiritual beliefs, or the historical trauma that affected her entire community.

"They wanted me to sit in circles and talk about my feelings," she told me, "but they weren't the right kind of circles. They didn't understand what healing means to my people."

Mary's observation cut straight to the heart of a crucial challenge: How do you integrate evidence-based therapeutic approaches like MI with indigenous healing traditions that have their own sophisticated understanding of wellness, change, and community support?

This isn't about choosing between Western and indigenous approaches. It's about creating respectful integration that honors traditional wisdom while offering additional resources that can support healing within cultural context.

The key is understanding that many indigenous communities have healing traditions that are far older and often more holistic than contemporary Western approaches. Our role isn't to replace these traditions but to support them and, when appropriate, offer complementary resources that align with rather than conflict with traditional healing frameworks.

Respecting Traditional Healing Practices and Worldviews

Indigenous healing traditions across North America share certain common elements while maintaining distinct tribal and cultural characteristics. Understanding these common frameworks helps you work respectfully within indigenous worldviews rather than imposing Western assumptions about health and healing.

Holistic Understanding of Wellness views health as balance between mental, physical, spiritual, and relational aspects of life. Problems aren't seen as individual pathology but as disruptions in this balance that affect the whole person within their community context.

This holistic perspective aligns beautifully with MI's emphasis on helping people find their own motivation for change rather than focusing solely on symptom reduction or behavioral modification.

Connection to Land and Nature isn't just environmental awareness—it's fundamental spiritual and psychological grounding that influences identity, healing practices, and understanding of human place in the world.

For many indigenous clients, disconnection from land and traditional territories contributes to psychological distress while reconnection supports healing and recovery.

Spiritual Dimensions of Problems and Healing integrate concepts that don't exist in Western psychological frameworks. Problems might be understood as spiritual imbalance, disconnection from cultural practices, or consequences of historical trauma that affects entire communities.

Healing might involve ceremony, prayer, connection with ancestors, or restoration of spiritual balance that requires traditional practices rather than or in addition to psychological interventions.

Community-Centered Approaches view individual problems within community context and emphasize collective support, cultural participation, and restoration of appropriate relationships rather than individual autonomy or self-reliance.

These community-centered approaches can seem to conflict with Western therapeutic emphasis on individual change and personal responsibility, but they actually offer sophisticated frameworks for supporting sustainable healing.

Understanding Historical Trauma and Cultural Genocide

Working with indigenous clients requires understanding the ongoing impact of historical trauma, cultural genocide, and intergenerational transmission of trauma that affects individuals, families, and entire communities.

Boarding School Legacy removed children from their families and communities, forbade native languages and cultural practices, and created intergenerational disruption of traditional parenting and cultural transmission.

Many contemporary indigenous adults are children or grandchildren of boarding school survivors who experienced severe trauma and cultural disruption that affects family functioning and cultural connection across generations.

Cultural Suppression and Criminalization made traditional healing practices, languages, and ceremonies illegal for decades, forcing indigenous communities to practice their traditions in secret or lose them entirely.

This suppression created additional trauma around cultural identity and traditional healing practices that influences contemporary attitudes toward seeking help and maintaining cultural connections.

Land Loss and Environmental Destruction severed connections to sacred sites, traditional territories, and natural resources that are essential for both physical survival and spiritual well-being.

The psychological impact of land loss extends far beyond economic consequences to include spiritual disconnection, cultural disruption, and loss of traditional healing resources.

Ongoing Discrimination and Marginalization continues to affect indigenous communities through systemic racism, economic inequality, inadequate healthcare and education, and ongoing threats to tribal sovereignty and cultural preservation.

Understanding these historical and contemporary realities helps you contextualize individual struggles within broader patterns of trauma and resilience rather than pathologizing cultural responses to systemic oppression.

Circle Processes and Community Involvement in Change

Many indigenous cultures use circle processes for decision-making, conflict resolution, and healing that can be integrated with or adapted for therapeutic purposes.

Talking Circles create sacred spaces for sharing experiences, expressing concerns, and receiving community support. The circular format emphasizes equality, shared responsibility, and collective wisdom rather than hierarchical expert-client relationships.

These processes align well with MI's collaborative spirit while providing culturally familiar frameworks for discussing problems and exploring change.

Healing Circles might include family members, community elders, traditional healers, and spiritual leaders who provide different types of support and guidance for people going through difficulties.

Understanding and working with existing healing circle traditions can enhance rather than compete with professional therapeutic services.

Decision-Making Circles involve community input into important choices affecting individuals or families. These processes can seem slow or inefficient from Western perspectives but they ensure that changes align with cultural values and have community support.

Rather than pushing for individual decision-making, you can help clients navigate appropriate circle processes while providing professional input that supports their cultural change mechanisms.

Incorporating Connection to Land, Ancestry, and Spirituality

Connection to land, ancestors, and spiritual traditions provides psychological and cultural resources that can support healing and recovery when integrated respectfully with professional services.

Land-Based Healing might involve time spent in traditional territories, participation in land-based traditional activities, or incorporation of natural elements into healing practices.

This doesn't mean you need to conduct therapy outdoors, but it does mean understanding and supporting client connections to land and nature as legitimate healing resources.

Ancestral Wisdom provides guidance through traditional stories, teachings passed down through generations, and spiritual connection with ancestors who faced similar challenges.

"What would your grandmother say about this situation?" isn't just a clinical question—it's accessing actual cultural wisdom that can provide guidance and strength for contemporary challenges.

Spiritual Practices might include smudging, prayer, ceremony, or other traditional practices that provide spiritual cleansing, protection, or guidance for healing processes.

Understanding and respecting these practices creates space for clients to integrate traditional healing with professional support rather than feeling forced to choose between different healing approaches.

Traditional Foods and Medicines represent both physical and cultural nourishment that can support healing when available and culturally appropriate.

Supporting client access to traditional foods and medicines (when legal and safe) honors cultural healing approaches while complementing professional treatment.

Case Study: Integrating Traditional and Contemporary Healing

Let me share a detailed example of how this integration worked with Robert, a 35-year-old member of the Lakota Nation who came to see me for depression and alcohol use problems.

Robert had grown up on the reservation but moved to the city for work opportunities. He felt disconnected from his cultural community and struggled with what he described as "spiritual emptiness" alongside his depression and drinking.

Previous treatment programs had focused on individual behavioral change without addressing his cultural identity or spiritual needs. Robert felt like these programs asked him to become someone else rather than helping him find his way back to who he was culturally and spiritually.

When we began working together, I started by acknowledging my limitations as a non-Native therapist and asking Robert to teach me about Lakota healing traditions that were important to him.

Robert shared that in Lakota culture, problems like his might be understood as spiritual imbalance requiring ceremony, community support, and reconnection with traditional practices. He had been thinking about participating in sweat lodge ceremonies but felt conflicted about whether this would conflict with professional treatment.

Instead of viewing traditional healing as competition for professional services, we explored how ceremony and cultural participation might support his recovery goals. Robert began attending sweat lodge ceremonies while also working with me on practical strategies for managing depression and reducing alcohol use.

Robert's healing process involved multiple elements: traditional ceremony for spiritual balance, community connection through cultural activities, professional therapy for depression management, and practical life changes to support sobriety.

Rather than choosing between traditional and contemporary approaches, Robert found that they complemented each other. The ceremony provided spiritual grounding and cultural connection that gave meaning to the practical changes he was making in therapy.

Six months later, Robert reported significant improvement in both depression and alcohol use. More importantly, he felt reconnected to his cultural identity and spiritual practices in ways that provided ongoing support for his recovery.

Working with Indigenous Families and Communities

Indigenous family structures often extend beyond nuclear family to include extended family, adopted family, and community relationships that provide support and guidance throughout life.

Extended Family Networks might include grandparents, aunts, uncles, and cousins who play active roles in child-rearing, decision-making, and support provision. These networks often continue traditional ways of sharing responsibility for family members' well-being.

Understanding these networks helps you identify resources and navigate change processes that honor existing family support systems rather than emphasizing individual autonomy over collective responsibility.

Clan and Tribal Relationships create additional layers of identity and belonging that influence individual functioning and community connections. People might have responsibilities to clan members and receive support from tribal community that extends beyond immediate family.

Traditional Gender and Age Roles might include specific responsibilities, privileges, and sources of guidance that influence how people understand their place in the community and their approaches to problem-solving.

These traditional roles aren't necessarily rigid or oppressive, but they do provide cultural context for understanding resistance, motivation, and goal-setting processes.

Community Leadership often includes traditional leaders, elders, and spiritual advisors who provide guidance for community members facing difficulties. These leaders might have their own approaches to helping people through challenges.

Working collaboratively with traditional community leaders (when appropriate and desired by clients) can enhance rather than compete with professional therapeutic services.

Addressing Substance Use from Indigenous Perspectives

Substance use problems in indigenous communities are often understood within frameworks of historical trauma, cultural disconnection, and spiritual imbalance rather than individual pathology or moral failure.

Historical Trauma Responses recognize that substance use might represent attempts to cope with intergenerational trauma, cultural loss, and ongoing discrimination that affect entire communities.

This perspective doesn't excuse harmful behavior, but it provides cultural context that influences how problems are understood and addressed.

Cultural Disconnection as a risk factor emphasizes how separation from traditional practices, communities, and cultural identity can contribute to vulnerability to substance use and other mental health problems.

Recovery might involve cultural reconnection as much as behavioral change, requiring access to traditional practices, community involvement, and cultural education.

Spiritual Imbalance frameworks view substance use as symptoms of disconnection from spiritual practices, traditional teachings, or appropriate relationship with the natural world.

Healing might require spiritual intervention through ceremony, traditional healing practices, or restoration of spiritual balance alongside practical changes in behavior.

Community-Based Recovery emphasizes collective support, cultural participation, and community accountability rather than individual treatment approaches that separate people from their cultural context.

Language and Cultural Expression

Many indigenous languages contain concepts and expressions that don't translate directly into English but carry important cultural and psychological meaning.

Native Language Processing might feel more natural and authentic for discussing cultural concepts, spiritual experiences, or traditional healing approaches.

Even clients who speak fluent English might prefer to use native language terms for cultural concepts or spiritual experiences that don't translate well into Western psychological language.

Storytelling Traditions provide frameworks for sharing experiences, teaching lessons, and processing difficulties that might feel more natural than direct question-and-answer therapeutic formats.

Understanding and working with traditional storytelling approaches can facilitate deeper therapeutic engagement while honoring cultural communication preferences.

Ceremonial Language might include prayers, songs, or ritual expressions that provide spiritual resources for healing and change processes.

Respecting and creating space for ceremonial language (when appropriate) shows cultural sensitivity while supporting client access to traditional spiritual resources.

Adapting MI Techniques for Indigenous Cultural Contexts

Standard MI techniques can be adapted to align with indigenous cultural values and healing traditions while maintaining the collaborative spirit that makes MI effective across cultures.

Reflective Listening can incorporate spiritual and community context. Instead of only reflecting individual emotions, you can reflect the cultural and spiritual dimensions of client experiences.

"It sounds like you're feeling disconnected not just from yourself but from your cultural community and spiritual practices" acknowledges the holistic nature of indigenous wellness.

Open-Ended Questions can explore cultural resources and traditional wisdom. "What do your elders say about healing from this kind of problem?" accesses cultural guidance while showing respect for traditional knowledge.

"How do your traditional teachings help you understand what you're going through?" identifies cultural resources that might support healing processes.

Affirmations can recognize both individual strengths and cultural identity. "Your connection to your cultural traditions is clearly important to you" affirms cultural values while supporting therapeutic engagement.

"It takes courage to seek healing through both traditional and contemporary approaches" validates the complex navigation required for bicultural healing processes.

Summaries can weave together individual goals, cultural values, and spiritual considerations without creating artificial conflicts between different healing approaches.

"You want to address this problem for your own well-being, but you're also thinking about how to honor your cultural teachings and reconnect with traditional practices that support healing. And you're trying to find ways to integrate both traditional and contemporary resources without having to choose between them."

These summaries honor the complexity of indigenous healing while maintaining focus on achievable change processes that respect cultural authenticity.

Working with Intergenerational Trauma Transmission

Intergenerational trauma affects indigenous families in ways that require understanding of how historical experiences continue to influence contemporary functioning across generations.

Trauma Transmission Patterns might include disrupted attachment, cultural loss, and learned survival strategies that were adaptive in traumatic contexts but create difficulties in contemporary situations.

Understanding these patterns helps you contextualize family dynamics and individual symptoms within broader historical frameworks rather than pathologizing culturally influenced behaviors.

Healing as Cultural Reclamation involves helping clients reconnect with cultural practices, languages, and traditions that were disrupted by historical trauma but can provide resources for contemporary healing.

This might involve supporting clients in learning traditional languages, participating in cultural activities, or connecting with tribal communities and cultural teachers.

Breaking Trauma Cycles requires both individual healing and cultural restoration that can provide healthier frameworks for future generations.

The goal isn't just symptom reduction but cultural healing that strengthens both individual recovery and community wellness.

Ceremonial and Ritual Integration

Many indigenous clients find strength and healing through traditional ceremonies and rituals that can complement professional therapeutic services when integrated respectfully.

Sweat Lodge Ceremonies provide purification, spiritual cleansing, and community support that can enhance therapeutic work by addressing spiritual dimensions of healing.

Vision Quests or Fasting offer traditional frameworks for seeking guidance, spiritual growth, and life direction that can complement therapeutic exploration of goals and values.

Smudging and Prayer create sacred space and spiritual protection that can support therapeutic processes while honoring cultural practices.

Seasonal Ceremonies connect healing with natural cycles and traditional calendar observances that provide cultural grounding and community participation.

Understanding and respecting these ceremonial practices creates opportunities for clients to integrate traditional healing with professional support rather than experiencing them as competing approaches.

Mental Health Stigma in Indigenous Communities

Mental health stigma in indigenous communities is complicated by historical trauma, cultural suppression, and ongoing discrimination that affect attitudes toward professional help-seeking.

Historical Trauma from Mental Health Systems includes forced institutionalization, cultural suppression in treatment settings, and professional practices that pathologized cultural differences rather than understanding them.

This history creates reasonable suspicion about professional mental health services that must be addressed through demonstrated cultural competence and respect.

Cultural Explanation Frameworks might view psychological distress as spiritual imbalance, cultural disconnection, or community problems rather than individual mental illness requiring professional treatment.

Understanding these frameworks helps you work within rather than against existing cultural understanding while offering professional resources that complement traditional approaches.

Community Protective Strategies might discourage sharing family or community problems with outsiders, especially non-Native professionals, to protect the community from negative judgments or harmful interventions.

Respecting these protective strategies while building trust through cultural competence and community connection creates opportunities for collaboration rather than competition with cultural values.

Creating Culturally Safe Therapeutic Environments

Cultural safety goes beyond cultural competence to create therapeutic environments where indigenous clients can express their cultural identity without fear of judgment, discrimination, or cultural suppression.

Sacred Space Creation might involve incorporating natural elements, allowing for smudging or prayer, or creating physical environments that feel welcoming to indigenous clients.

This doesn't mean appropriating indigenous symbols or practices, but it does mean creating space for clients to bring their cultural identity into the therapeutic relationship.

Cultural Symbol Respect involves understanding and honoring the meaning of cultural objects, practices, or symbols that clients might bring into therapy while maintaining appropriate boundaries around sacred practices.

Family and Community Inclusion creates opportunities for traditional support systems to participate in healing processes when appropriate and desired by clients.

This might involve family meetings, community circles, or collaboration with traditional healers and cultural leaders.

Training and Supervision Considerations

Working effectively with indigenous clients requires specialized training, ongoing cultural learning, and supervision that addresses the unique challenges of cross-cultural therapeutic work.

Historical Education about specific tribal histories, traditional healing practices, and the impact of colonization provides essential context for understanding contemporary indigenous experiences.

Cultural Consultation with indigenous professionals, traditional healers, or community leaders helps ensure that therapeutic approaches are culturally appropriate and respectful.

Ongoing Relationship Building with indigenous communities creates opportunities for cultural learning, professional collaboration, and community trust-building that enhances clinical effectiveness.

Supervision Focus should include regular attention to cultural dynamics, power differences, and the intersection of individual therapy with community healing processes.

Advocacy and Systems Change

Working with indigenous clients often involves advocacy and systems change efforts that address the structural barriers and historical injustices that contribute to individual psychological distress.

Healthcare Access advocacy might involve working to improve indigenous access to culturally appropriate mental health services, traditional healing resources, and integrated care approaches.

Cultural Preservation support might include advocating for language revitalization programs, traditional healing practice protection, and cultural education resources that support community wellness.

Historical Justice work might involve supporting efforts to address historical injustices, recover stolen lands or artifacts, or obtain recognition and reparations for historical trauma.

Professional Education advocacy might include working to improve cultural competence training for mental health professionals and increase indigenous representation in mental health professions.

What This Means for Your Practice

Working effectively with indigenous clients requires deep respect for cultural traditions combined with commitment to ongoing cultural learning and community relationship-building.

Cultural Humility becomes essential rather than optional. Approach each indigenous client as a teacher about their cultural traditions while offering professional resources that can complement rather than compete with traditional healing approaches.

Traditional Healing Integration requires learning about and respecting indigenous healing traditions while finding ways to offer professional services that enhance rather than replace cultural resources.

Community Connection involves building relationships with indigenous communities, traditional healers, and cultural leaders that can support collaborative approaches to individual and community healing.

Historical Trauma Understanding provides essential context for individual symptoms and family dynamics while informing therapeutic approaches that address both historical and contemporary sources of distress.

Advocacy Commitment extends beyond individual therapy to include systems change efforts that address the structural barriers and historical injustices that contribute to indigenous mental health disparities.

Most importantly, approach each indigenous client with genuine respect for their cultural expertise while offering professional resources that can support their own healing goals within their cultural context.

When you can work skillfully within indigenous cultural frameworks while maintaining MI's collaborative spirit, you create therapeutic relationships that honor both individual healing and cultural wisdom. That's not just culturally responsive therapy—it's healing work that supports both personal recovery and cultural revitalization.

The Path Forward

Indigenous approaches to healing offer sophisticated frameworks for understanding wellness, change, and community support that can enrich rather than conflict with contemporary therapeutic approaches. The key is approaching this integration with genuine respect, cultural humility, and commitment to ongoing learning.

This work isn't easy, and it's not something you can master through reading or training alone. It requires relationship-building with indigenous communities, ongoing cultural learning, and willingness to have your assumptions challenged by indigenous wisdom and experience.

But for indigenous clients who have often felt misunderstood or culturally invalidated by previous professional experiences, this integrated approach can provide healing opportunities that honor both their cultural identity and their individual needs for support and change.

That's not just good therapy—it's cultural healing work that supports both individual recovery and the broader project of indigenous cultural survival and revitalization that benefits entire communities.

Chapter 8: Middle Eastern Perspectives

Faith, Family, and Decision-Making

When Fatima first came to see me, she brought her hijab, her five daily prayers, her extended family's expectations, and her husband's cautious permission to seek professional help. She also brought her own quiet strength, her university education, her fluent English, and her determination to find a way through the depression that had been affecting her for months.

Fatima's situation illustrates the complexity that many Middle Eastern clients navigate in therapy: deep religious faith that provides both comfort and constraint, family systems that offer support while expecting conformity, and cultural values that emphasize community harmony while they struggle with individual needs for change and growth.

Working effectively with Middle Eastern clients requires understanding how Islamic principles, family honor, and traditional decision-making processes influence every aspect of the therapeutic relationship. This doesn't mean making assumptions about individual religious practice or family dynamics, but it does mean being prepared to work respectfully within these cultural frameworks when they're important to clients.

The key insight is that Middle Eastern cultures often integrate faith, family, and community in ways that Western therapeutic approaches might not immediately understand or accommodate. Successful MI with Middle Eastern clients involves working within these integrated systems rather than trying to separate individual motivation from religious and family contexts.

Islamic Principles and Their Intersection with MI

Islam provides a comprehensive framework for understanding life's challenges, personal growth, and community relationships that can either support or complicate therapeutic work, depending on how well therapeutic approaches align with Islamic values and teachings.

Tawhid (the unity and oneness of Allah) influences how practicing Muslims understand the interconnectedness of all aspects of life. Mental health, family relationships, work, and spiritual practice aren't separate categories—they're integrated aspects of a unified existence under God's guidance.

This integrated perspective aligns well with holistic therapeutic approaches but can create tension with Western psychology's tendency to compartmentalize different aspects of functioning.

Qadar (divine predestination) represents the Islamic teaching that Allah has knowledge and control over all events, which can influence how Muslims understand personal agency, responsibility, and the possibility of change.

Some clients might struggle with therapeutic emphasis on personal choice and behavior modification if they believe their difficulties are divinely ordained or if they feel that accepting professional help demonstrates insufficient faith in Allah's plan.

Working with these beliefs requires understanding how to support personal responsibility and change efforts within the framework of divine sovereignty rather than creating theological conflicts.

Tawakkul (trust in Allah) encourages believers to make appropriate effort while trusting in Allah's wisdom and timing. This principle can support therapeutic work by encouraging active engagement while reducing anxiety about outcomes.

"Make your effort and trust in Allah" becomes a framework for approaching change that honors both individual responsibility and spiritual surrender.

Sabr (patience and perseverance) is highly valued in Islamic tradition and can provide cultural resources for tolerating difficult emotions, working through long-term change processes, and maintaining hope during challenging periods.

Understanding and working with the concept of *sabr* can help clients find cultural and spiritual resources for sustaining motivation through difficult therapeutic work.

Understanding Islamic Approaches to Mental Health

Islamic tradition has its own sophisticated understanding of mental health, emotional well-being, and healing that predates and sometimes conflicts with Western psychological approaches.

Spiritual Dimensions of Psychological Distress might be understood as tests from Allah, consequences of spiritual neglect, or opportunities for spiritual growth rather than pathological conditions requiring medical intervention.

This doesn't mean dismissing the reality of mental health symptoms, but it does mean understanding how clients might interpret their experiences within religious frameworks that emphasize spiritual rather than psychological explanations.

Prayer and Dhikr (remembrance of Allah) provide traditional resources for managing anxiety, depression, and emotional distress through spiritual practices that connect believers with divine support and guidance.

Understanding and supporting these spiritual practices can complement rather than compete with therapeutic interventions while honoring client religious commitments.

Community Support and Religious Obligations create networks of mutual assistance and spiritual accountability that can provide resources for mental health recovery when integrated appropriately with professional treatment.

Halal and Haram considerations influence what kinds of therapeutic approaches and lifestyle changes feel religiously permissible to observant Muslim clients.

Understanding these religious boundaries helps you avoid recommending interventions that create spiritual conflicts while finding religiously compatible approaches to therapeutic goals.

Family Honor and Collective Decision-Making

Middle Eastern family systems often operate on principles of collective honor, intergenerational responsibility, and group decision-making that can seem to conflict with Western therapeutic emphasis on individual autonomy and self-determination.

Family Honor (*sharaf* in Arabic, *abru* in Persian) represents the collective reputation and social standing of the entire extended family, which can be affected by individual members' behavior, choices, and problems.

When clients seek therapy, they might be concerned not just about their individual well-being but about how their problems or treatment might affect their family's standing in the community.

This creates therapeutic dynamics where individual change must be considered within the context of family impact and community perception.

Intergenerational Authority typically gives significant decision-making power to elders, parents, and senior family members whose approval might be necessary for major life changes or treatment decisions.

Understanding these authority structures helps you work within rather than against existing family systems while still supporting individual agency and growth.

Collective Decision-Making might require family consultation, elder input, or community consensus before individuals feel comfortable committing to significant behavior changes or life modifications.

Rather than viewing this as unhealthy dependence, you can understand it as cultural norm that ensures changes align with family values and have community support.

Gender-Specific Roles and Expectations influence what kinds of problems can be discussed openly, what kinds of solutions are considered appropriate, and what kinds of changes align with cultural expectations for men and women.

Case Study: Working Within Islamic and Family Frameworks

Ahmad was a 30-year-old Palestinian American man who came to see me for anxiety that was affecting his work performance and family relationships. He was married with two young children, worked as an engineer, and was active in his mosque community.

Ahmad's anxiety seemed connected to pressure he felt as the primary breadwinner for his nuclear family while also supporting his aging parents financially. He felt caught between American expectations for individual achievement and Palestinian cultural expectations for family loyalty and support.

When we began exploring his concerns, Ahmad was clear that any solutions needed to align with his Islamic faith and honor his family obligations. He wasn't interested in therapeutic approaches that would require him to prioritize individual needs over family responsibilities or that would conflict with his religious beliefs.

Instead of framing this as resistance to change, I worked within his value system to explore how he might manage anxiety while still fulfilling his cultural and religious obligations.

We discussed Islamic teachings about balance, the importance of taking care of one's own health in order to serve others effectively, and how excessive anxiety might actually interfere with his ability to be the kind of husband, father, and son his faith called him to be.

Ahmad found motivation for anxiety management in his desire to be a better Muslim, husband, and father rather than in purely individual goals for stress reduction. His religious faith became a resource for change rather than an obstacle to therapeutic work.

We also explored how to have conversations with his family about the pressures he was experiencing. Rather than demanding individual space or reduced obligations, Ahmad learned to communicate about his stress in ways that showed continued commitment to family values while asking for understanding and support.

The anxiety improvement came not through reduced family involvement but through better integration of individual self-care with family and religious responsibilities. Ahmad's faith community also became a source of support once he learned to talk about mental health in religiously compatible ways.

Gender Considerations in MI Practice

Traditional Middle Eastern cultures often have specific expectations and constraints around gender roles that influence how men and women express problems, seek help, and consider change options.

Male Role Expectations might emphasize strength, family leadership, emotional control, and responsibility for family honor. These expectations can make it particularly challenging for Middle Eastern men to acknowledge vulnerability, seek professional help, or express emotional distress.

Working with Middle Eastern men might require approaches that honor cultural expectations while still addressing underlying concerns. Framing therapy as consultation or education rather than emotional healing can make the process feel more culturally appropriate.

Female Role Expectations might emphasize family harmony, modesty, and deference to male family members' authority. Middle Eastern women might need family permission to seek therapy or might feel conflicted about prioritizing individual well-being over family needs.

Understanding these role expectations helps you work within cultural constraints while still supporting individual growth and empowerment.

Gender-Segregated Therapeutic Relationships might be necessary or strongly preferred by some clients based on religious beliefs about appropriate interaction between men and women.

Being prepared to provide same-gender therapeutic services or make appropriate referrals shows respect for religious requirements while ensuring that clients can access help within their comfort zones.

Family Decision-Making Involving Gender Dynamics might require understanding how traditional authority structures work in specific families and how to include appropriate family members in therapeutic discussions without violating cultural or religious boundaries.

Working with Religious Leaders and Community Structures

Islamic communities often have religious and community leadership structures that can provide support for therapeutic work when approached respectfully and appropriately.

Imam Relationships with local religious leaders can provide spiritual guidance, religious consultation, and community support that complement professional therapeutic services.

Understanding when and how to involve religious leaders requires sensitivity to client preferences, religious boundaries, and appropriate professional collaboration.

Mosque Community Support can provide social connection, spiritual resources, and practical assistance that support therapeutic goals while maintaining cultural and religious grounding.

Islamic Counseling Traditions exist within many communities and might include religiously-based approaches to problem-solving that can complement or provide alternatives to secular therapeutic approaches.

Understanding these existing resources prevents competition between professional and religious helping while creating opportunities for integrated support.

Halal Therapeutic Approaches ensure that therapeutic interventions align with Islamic principles and don't create religious conflicts for observant Muslim clients.

This might influence everything from therapeutic techniques to scheduling considerations to family involvement in treatment.

Language and Cultural Expression

Arabic language and cultural concepts shape how many Middle Eastern clients understand and express psychological experiences in ways that don't always translate directly into Western psychological terminology.

Arabic Emotional Vocabulary includes concepts like *ghalaba* (being overwhelmed), *za'al* (hurt feelings), and *qahr* (suppressed anger) that have cultural nuances that simple translation might miss.

Understanding these concepts helps you work within rather than against existing cultural frameworks for understanding emotional experience.

Religious Language Integration might include Arabic phrases, Quranic references, or Islamic concepts that provide meaning and comfort within therapeutic conversations.

Being familiar with basic Islamic concepts and comfortable with religious language shows respect while facilitating deeper therapeutic engagement.

Family Communication Patterns might include different levels of directness, different authority relationships, and different boundaries around emotional expression that reflect cultural rather than pathological dynamics.

Code-Switching Challenges affect many Middle Eastern Americans who navigate between traditional family contexts and mainstream American environments that require different communication styles and behavioral expectations.

Understanding and normalizing these cultural adaptations helps clients develop comfort with cultural flexibility rather than feeling torn between different cultural worlds.

Religious Practices as Therapeutic Resources

Islamic religious practices can provide powerful resources for mental health recovery when understood and integrated appropriately with professional therapeutic approaches.

Five Daily Prayers create structure, mindfulness opportunities, and spiritual connection that can support anxiety management, depression recovery, and general emotional regulation.

Understanding how to work with rather than around prayer schedules shows respect while potentially enhancing therapeutic effectiveness.

Ramadan Fasting provides annual practice in self-discipline, spiritual reflection, and community solidarity that can be connected to therapeutic goals around impulse control, mindfulness, and social support.

Zakat (charitable giving) and community service create opportunities for meaningful activity, social connection, and spiritual growth that can support recovery from depression and other mental health challenges.

Hajj and Umrah pilgrimages provide spiritual experiences and community connections that might influence therapeutic timing, goals, or resource identification.

Addressing Mental Health Stigma in Middle Eastern Communities

Mental health stigma in Middle Eastern communities is influenced by cultural values around family honor, religious explanations for distress, and historical experiences with Western psychological approaches that didn't understand Islamic or cultural frameworks.

Individual Problems as Family Shame means that seeking professional help might feel like public admission of family failure or inadequate religious faith.

Understanding these concerns helps you work with rather than against family protective strategies while providing necessary individual support.

Religious Explanations for Distress might emphasize spiritual rather than psychological solutions, creating potential conflicts between religious and professional approaches to healing.

Working collaboratively with religious frameworks rather than competing with them creates opportunities for integrated healing that honors both spiritual and psychological needs.

Cultural Solutions First might include trying religious resources, family consultation, or traditional healing approaches before considering professional intervention.

Respecting these cultural approaches while offering professional support creates complementary rather than competing healing resources.

Adapting MI Techniques for Middle Eastern Cultural Contexts

Standard MI techniques can be modified to align with Middle Eastern cultural and religious values while maintaining the collaborative spirit that makes MI effective across cultures.

Reflective Listening can incorporate religious and family contexts. Instead of only reflecting individual emotions, you can reflect the spiritual and cultural dimensions of client experiences.

"You're trying to balance taking care of yourself with your responsibilities to your family and your faith" acknowledges the integrated nature of Middle Eastern decision-making.

Open-Ended Questions can explore religious resources and family wisdom. "What does your faith teach about dealing with this kind of challenge?" accesses religious guidance while showing respect for Islamic teachings.

"How do you think your family would want you to handle this situation?" honors collective decision-making while gathering information about family support and expectations.

Affirmations can recognize both individual strengths and cultural values. "Your commitment to your faith is clearly important to you" affirms religious priorities while supporting therapeutic engagement.

"It's clear that your family relationships are a source of strength for you" validates cultural values that can anchor therapeutic work.

Summaries can weave together individual concerns, family considerations, and religious principles without creating artificial conflicts between different value systems.

"You want to address this concern for your own well-being, but you also want to make sure any changes align with your Islamic beliefs and honor your family relationships. And you're looking for approaches that integrate all these important parts of your life."

Working with Immigrant and Refugee Experiences

Many Middle Eastern clients in Western countries are immigrants or refugees who navigate additional layers of cultural adaptation, potential trauma, and acculturation stress.

Immigration Stress includes language barriers, economic challenges, cultural adaptation pressure, and often separation from extended family and community support systems.

Refugee Trauma might include war exposure, displacement, family separation, and ongoing concerns about safety and legal status that significantly impact mental health.

Acculturation Conflicts emerge when traditional Middle Eastern values seem to conflict with Western expectations around individual autonomy, gender roles, or religious practice.

Discrimination and Islamophobia create additional stress and trauma that affect mental health while also influencing attitudes toward seeking help from Western professional systems.

Understanding these multiple layers of stress helps you contextualize individual symptoms within broader patterns of cultural adaptation and survival.

What This Means for Your Practice

Working effectively with Middle Eastern clients requires genuine respect for Islamic and cultural values combined with flexibility in therapeutic approaches that honor religious and family frameworks.

Religious Sensitivity becomes essential rather than optional. Learn basic Islamic concepts, show respect for religious practices, and be prepared to work within rather than against religious frameworks.

Family System Understanding helps you navigate collective decision-making processes while still supporting individual growth and change within appropriate cultural contexts.

Cultural Humility about Middle Eastern history, politics, and contemporary experiences prevents assumptions while creating space for clients to educate you about their specific cultural and religious backgrounds.

Integration Approaches that combine professional resources with religious and cultural supports create more effective and culturally authentic therapeutic relationships than approaches that compete with existing value systems.

Community Connection involves understanding and respecting the religious and cultural communities that provide meaning, support, and guidance for Middle Eastern clients.

Most importantly, approach each Middle Eastern client as an individual with their own unique relationship to Islamic faith, cultural traditions, and family expectations. Religious and cultural knowledge provides important context, but individual assessment and respect for personal experience remain essential.

When you can work skillfully within Middle Eastern cultural and religious contexts while maintaining MI's collaborative spirit, you create therapeutic relationships that honor faith, family, and individual well-being simultaneously. That's not just culturally responsive therapy—it's healing work that supports both personal growth and cultural authenticity within religious frameworks that provide meaning and guidance.

Chapter 9: LGBTQ+ Affirmation

Identity-Affirming Motivational Conversations

When Marcus walked into my office, he carried two decades of hiding, three failed attempts at conversion therapy, and one fragile hope that maybe—finally—he could find a way to be both gay and okay with himself. He'd grown up in a conservative Christian family where being gay was seen as sinful, shameful, and something that needed to be fixed or hidden.

"I don't know if I can change who I am," he told me in our first session, "but I'm tired of hating myself for it."

Marcus's struggle illustrates the complex therapeutic territory that LGBTQ+ clients often navigate: the intersection of identity, family relationships, community belonging, and personal well-being in contexts where sexual and gender identities might not be accepted or supported.

Working with LGBTQ+ clients using MI requires understanding how identity development, internalized stigma, family dynamics, and minority stress influence every aspect of the therapeutic relationship. It also requires moving beyond neutral or tolerant approaches to actively affirming LGBTQ+ identities while supporting clients in their own identity exploration and integration processes.

The key insight is that for LGBTQ+ clients, therapeutic work isn't just about changing problematic behaviors or managing symptoms—it's often about discovering, accepting, and integrating authentic identity in contexts that might not support or celebrate that authenticity.

This means MI with LGBTQ+ clients must be explicitly affirming rather than neutral, must understand minority stress as a legitimate source of mental health concerns, and must support identity development as a therapeutic goal rather than treating sexual and gender identity as tangential to other therapeutic work.

Creating Safe Spaces for Identity Exploration

Before any meaningful therapeutic work can happen with LGBTQ+ clients, you must establish psychological safety around sexual and gender identity. Many LGBTQ+ individuals have experienced rejection, discrimination, or conversion attempts from previous helpers, making initial trust-building crucial.

Explicit Affirmation goes beyond generic statements about accepting all clients to specifically affirming LGBTQ+ identities as healthy, natural, and valuable. This might include affirming statements in intake materials, rainbow symbols in office spaces, or direct verbal affirmation early in therapeutic relationships.

"I want you to know that I view LGBTQ+ identities as healthy and normal variations of human experience, and my goal is to support you in becoming who you authentically are, not to change your sexual orientation or gender identity."

Identity-Neutral Language until clients identify their own terms shows respect for the complexity and fluidity of sexual and gender identity. Use the language clients use to describe themselves rather than making assumptions based on appearance or relationships.

Coming Out Process Respect understands that identity development is ongoing rather than a one-time event. Clients might be at different stages of self-acceptance, social disclosure, or identity integration, and therapeutic goals should match their current developmental needs rather than pushing toward predetermined outcomes.

Safety Assessment becomes crucial when working with LGBTQ+ clients who might face family rejection, employment discrimination, housing instability, or physical violence related to their identity disclosure.

Understanding these real-world risks helps you support authentic identity expression while ensuring clients have adequate safety and support resources.

Understanding Minority Stress and Its Impact

Minority stress theory explains how chronic discrimination, prejudice, and stigma create unique mental health risks for LGBTQ+ individuals that go beyond general life stress to include identity-specific stressors.

Distal Stressors include external experiences of discrimination, violence, rejection, and prejudice that LGBTQ+ individuals face from families, communities, institutions, and society at large.

These stressors might include workplace discrimination, family rejection, religious condemnation, healthcare discrimination, or physical violence that create trauma and ongoing hypervigilance.

Proximal Stressors include internalized negative attitudes about LGBTQ+ identity, concealment efforts, and anticipation of rejection that create internal psychological stress even in the absence of actual discrimination.

These internal stressors often develop as protective responses to external discrimination but can continue to create distress even in supportive environments.

Intersectional Stressors affect LGBTQ+ individuals who also belong to other marginalized groups and face multiple, intersecting forms of discrimination based on race, religion, disability, socioeconomic status, or other identities.

Understanding these multiple layers of stress helps you contextualize client symptoms and therapeutic goals within broader patterns of social oppression rather than individual pathology.

Addressing Internalized Stigma and Shame

Many LGBTQ+ clients come to therapy carrying internalized negative messages about their sexual or gender identity that were learned from families, religious communities, or broader society.

Religious Trauma affects many LGBTQ+ individuals who grew up in faith communities that taught that their identities were sinful, shameful, or fundamentally wrong.

This religious trauma can create profound conflicts between spiritual needs and identity authenticity that require careful therapeutic navigation.

Family Message Internalization includes negative attitudes about LGBTQ+ identity learned from family members who expressed disappointment, shame, or rejection about sexual or gender diversity.

These family messages often become internalized self-criticism that interferes with healthy identity development and self-acceptance.

Societal Stigma Integration happens when LGBTQ+ individuals absorb broader cultural messages about heterosexual and cisgender superiority that position LGBTQ+ identities as inferior, abnormal, or undesirable.

Working with internalized stigma requires helping clients identify, challenge, and replace negative self-talk with affirming, realistic perspectives about LGBTQ+ identity and experience.

Case Study: Identity-Affirming MI in Practice

Let me share a detailed example of how identity-affirming MI worked with Sarah, a 25-year-old woman who came to therapy struggling with anxiety and depression following her recent realization that she was attracted to women.

Sarah had grown up in a conservative religious family and had been married to a man for three years. She loved her husband but felt increasingly disconnected from her marriage and confused about her sexual identity.

When Sarah first came to see me, she was careful to frame her concerns in terms of marital problems rather than sexual identity questions. She talked about feeling "different" and "wrong" without initially naming her attraction to women.

Rather than pushing for premature disclosure, I created space for identity exploration by affirming that sexual identity development is a normal part of human experience and that whatever she was discovering about herself was okay to discuss.

As trust built, Sarah began sharing her attraction to women and her confusion about what this meant for her marriage, her faith, and her family relationships. She was terrified of being rejected by her family and losing her community if she acknowledged her lesbian identity.

We worked together to separate her authentic feelings from her fears about consequences. Sarah's attraction to women wasn't the problem—the problem was living in a context where authentic identity felt dangerous.

I affirmed her lesbian identity as healthy and natural while helping her think through the practical challenges of living authentically in her current context. We explored how to honor her authentic self while making informed decisions about disclosure, marriage, and family relationships.

Sarah found her own reasons for authenticity: she wanted to be honest with her husband, she wanted to model authenticity for future children, and she wanted to live in alignment with her values of integrity and self-respect.

The therapy process supported Sarah's coming out to herself, her husband, and eventually her family. While these conversations were difficult, Sarah felt supported to navigate them authentically rather than continuing to hide her true identity.

Six months later, Sarah had ended her marriage amicably, was exploring dating women, and had found a supportive LGBTQ+ faith community. Most importantly, she reported feeling authentic and integrated for the first time in her adult life.

Family Dynamics and Coming Out Processes

LGBTQ+ clients often face complex family dynamics around identity disclosure that can include rejection, conditional acceptance, or gradual adjustment processes that affect mental health and therapeutic goals.

Parental Reactions to LGBTQ+ identity disclosure range from immediate acceptance to complete rejection, with many families going through adjustment processes that might include grief, anger, bargaining, or gradual acceptance.

Understanding these family adjustment processes helps you support clients through family responses while maintaining appropriate therapeutic boundaries around family work versus individual therapy.

Sibling Relationships might be affected differently by LGBTQ+ identity disclosure, with some siblings providing support while others struggle with acceptance or feel caught between LGBTQ+ siblings and disapproving parents.

Extended Family Dynamics can create additional complexity when clients have supportive immediate family but rejecting extended family, or when cultural or religious extended family influences create pressure on immediate family members.

Chosen Family Development becomes important when biological families aren't supportive, as LGBTQ+ clients often create "chosen families" of supportive friends, partners, and community members who provide the acceptance and belonging that biological families might not offer.

Understanding and supporting both biological family navigation and chosen family development helps clients build adequate support systems for identity integration and mental health recovery.

Working with Religious and Spiritual Conflicts

Many LGBTQ+ clients struggle with conflicts between their sexual or gender identity and their religious or spiritual beliefs, having been taught that they must choose between faith and authenticity.

Religious Trauma Recovery involves helping clients heal from harmful religious messages about LGBTQ+ identity while potentially maintaining connection to spiritual resources and communities that support their whole identity.

This doesn't mean choosing between faith and identity but finding ways to integrate both authentic identity and spiritual needs when possible.

Affirming Faith Communities exist within most religious traditions and can provide spiritual resources and community connection for LGBTQ+ individuals who want to maintain religious practice while living authentically.

Helping clients locate these affirming communities can resolve conflicts between faith and identity that seemed impossible to navigate.

Spiritual Resource Development might involve exploring LGBTQ+-affirming spiritual practices, finding religious leaders who support identity authenticity, or developing personal spiritual practices that integrate rather than conflict with sexual and gender identity.

Family Religious Conflicts emerge when clients want to maintain family relationships but face religious-based rejection or pressure to change their identity to remain connected to religious family members.

Working with these conflicts requires understanding religious frameworks while affirming LGBTQ+ identity and helping clients find ways to honor both their authentic selves and their family relationships when possible.

Gender Identity and Transgender Experiences

Transgender and gender non-conforming clients face unique challenges related to gender identity development, social transition, medical transition decisions, and family and community acceptance.

Gender Identity Development is often a gradual process of self-discovery that might include questioning, exploration, and integration phases that require different kinds of therapeutic support.

Understanding these developmental processes helps you support clients at their current stage rather than pushing toward predetermined outcomes about gender expression or transition decisions.

Social Transition Considerations include decisions about name changes, pronoun use, clothing, social role changes, and identity disclosure that can significantly impact safety, relationships, and mental health.

Supporting social transition decisions requires understanding both the benefits of authentic expression and the real-world risks that transgender individuals face in different contexts.

Medical Transition Questions might include hormone therapy, surgery, or other medical interventions that can support gender identity integration but also involve complex medical, financial, and social considerations.

Your role is to support informed decision-making rather than advocating for or against specific medical interventions, while ensuring clients have accurate information and appropriate medical resources.

Family and Community Response to transgender identity can be particularly challenging, as gender transition often requires more visible changes that affect how others perceive and interact with the person.

Understanding and preparing for these social responses helps transgender clients navigate transition processes with appropriate support and safety planning.

Intersectionality Considerations

LGBTQ+ individuals who also belong to other marginalized groups face multiple, intersecting forms of discrimination that create unique therapeutic challenges and resource needs.

Race and Sexual/Gender Identity Intersections create specific experiences for LGBTQ+ people of color who might face discrimination within both LGBTQ+ communities and racial/ethnic communities while also navigating broader societal racism and heterosexism.

Religious and Cultural Identity Intersections affect LGBTQ+ individuals from religious or cultural backgrounds where sexual and gender diversity aren't accepted, creating conflicts between cultural belonging and identity authenticity.

Socioeconomic Intersections influence access to LGBTQ+-affirming resources, healthcare, safe housing, and supportive communities that can significantly impact mental health and transition processes.

Disability and LGBTQ+ Identity Intersections create unique challenges around accessing LGBTQ+ communities and resources, navigating healthcare systems, and managing multiple forms of social marginalization.

Understanding these intersecting identities helps you provide culturally responsive care that addresses the full complexity of clients' experiences rather than focusing solely on sexual or gender identity.

Adapting MI Techniques for LGBTQ+ Affirmation

Standard MI techniques can be modified to explicitly affirm LGBTQ+ identity while maintaining the collaborative spirit that makes MI effective across diverse populations.

Reflective Listening can incorporate identity affirmation and minority stress validation. Instead of only reflecting emotions, you can reflect the courage and authenticity involved in LGBTQ+ identity development.

"It sounds like you're discovering important things about who you are, and that's both exciting and scary given how your family might react" validates both identity development and realistic concerns about consequences.

Open-Ended Questions can explore identity development and authenticity goals. "What does living authentically mean to you?" invites exploration of identity integration goals.

"How do you want to honor both your true self and your important relationships?" acknowledges the complexity of balancing authenticity with family and community connections.

Affirmations can explicitly celebrate LGBTQ+ identity and coming out courage. "It takes tremendous bravery to be honest about who you are in a world that doesn't always support that honesty" affirms both identity and courage.

"Your commitment to living authentically is really admirable" supports identity integration as a therapeutic value and goal.

Summaries can weave together identity development, safety considerations, and relationship impacts without suggesting that authenticity and safety are mutually exclusive.

"You're discovering important things about your identity and you want to live authentically, but you're also thinking carefully about how to do that safely and in ways that preserve the relationships that matter most to you."

Coming Out Support and Safety Planning

Coming out processes require careful planning that balances authenticity with safety, relationship preservation, and practical considerations that vary dramatically across different life contexts.

Safety Assessment becomes crucial before supporting any identity disclosure, as LGBTQ+ individuals can face employment discrimination, housing loss, family rejection, or physical violence following identity disclosure.

Understanding local laws, workplace policies, family dynamics, and community attitudes helps you support informed coming out decisions rather than encouraging disclosure without adequate safety planning.

Gradual Disclosure Processes often work better than dramatic revelation approaches, allowing clients to test reactions, build support systems, and maintain some control over the pace and scope of identity disclosure.

Support System Development might need to happen before or alongside coming out processes, as existing support systems might not be available after identity disclosure.

Helping clients identify and cultivate supportive relationships provides security for identity integration processes.

Financial and Practical Considerations influence coming out timing and safety for clients who might face employment discrimination, loss of family financial support, or housing instability following identity disclosure.

Building LGBTQ+ Community Connections

Connection to LGBTQ+ community provides crucial resources for identity development, social support, and mental health recovery that isolated LGBTQ+ individuals often lack.

Community Resource Education helps clients learn about local LGBTQ+ organizations, social groups, support services, and cultural events that can provide connection and belonging.

Online Community Access can provide support and connection for LGBTQ+ individuals in areas without strong local LGBTQ+ communities or for those who aren't ready for in-person community involvement.

Mentorship Connections with other LGBTQ+ individuals who have navigated similar identity development or life challenges can provide guidance and hope for clients who feel isolated or uncertain about their future.

Professional Network Development connects LGBTQ+ clients with affirming healthcare providers, legal resources, and professional services that understand and support LGBTQ+ needs.

What This Means for Your Practice

Working effectively with LGBTQ+ clients requires explicit affirmation, minority stress understanding, and identity development support rather than neutral or pathologizing approaches.

Explicit LGBTQ+ Affirmation becomes a therapeutic stance rather than optional accommodation. Your office environment, intake materials, and therapeutic language should clearly communicate LGBTQ+ support and celebration.

Minority Stress Education helps you understand how discrimination and stigma contribute to mental health symptoms while avoiding pathologizing LGBTQ+ identity itself.

Identity Development Support makes authentic identity exploration and integration legitimate therapeutic goals rather than tangential concerns to address alongside "real" mental health issues.

Safety-Informed Practice balances authenticity support with realistic assessment of discrimination risks and safety planning for identity disclosure and community participation.

Intersectional Awareness ensures that you understand how multiple identities interact to create unique experiences and therapeutic needs for LGBTQ+ clients with complex identity intersections.

Most importantly, approach each LGBTQ+ client as an expert in their own identity experience while offering professional support that affirms rather than questions the validity and healthiness of sexual and gender diversity.

When you can work skillfully within LGBTQ+ identity frameworks while maintaining MI's collaborative spirit, you create therapeutic relationships that support both identity integration and mental health recovery. That's not just LGBTQ+-affirming therapy—it's identity-affirming healing work that supports both personal authenticity and community belonging.

Looking Forward

LGBTQ+ affirmative therapy represents a fundamental shift from pathologizing approaches to identity-celebrating frameworks that view sexual and gender diversity as natural human variations deserving of support and celebration.

This approach requires ongoing education, self-examination, and commitment to social justice that extends beyond individual therapy to include advocacy for LGBTQ+ rights and community support.

But for LGBTQ+ clients who have often experienced rejection or conversion attempts from previous helpers, this affirmative approach can provide healing opportunities that support both mental health recovery and authentic identity integration.

That's not just good therapy—it's identity-affirming work that supports both individual healing and broader LGBTQ+ community health and resilience.

Section III: Practical Strategies

Chapter 10: Nonverbal Communication Across Cultures

Dr. Patel sat across from me with his hands folded neatly in his lap, eyes focused somewhere just past my left shoulder, nodding politely at everything I said. Using standard Western therapeutic assumptions, I might have concluded he was disengaged, avoiding connection, or being passive-aggressive about the therapy process.

But Dr. Patel wasn't doing any of those things. He was showing appropriate respect by avoiding direct eye contact with someone he perceived as having higher status. His folded hands demonstrated self-control and attentiveness. His indirect gaze was cultural courtesy, not avoidance. And his polite nodding reflected his upbringing in a culture where disagreeing openly with professionals would be considered rude.

I learned this the hard way after several sessions of trying to "engage" him more directly, which only made him more uncomfortable. Once I understood the cultural meaning behind his nonverbal behavior, everything changed. I adjusted my own body language to match his cultural expectations, and suddenly we had a much more authentic therapeutic relationship.

This experience taught me that nonverbal communication isn't universal. Every gesture, every pause, every spatial arrangement carries cultural meaning that can either support or undermine therapeutic relationships. What feels warm and engaging to someone from one culture might feel intrusive or disrespectful to someone from another.

MI practitioners need to become fluent in this silent language of culture, learning to read nonverbal cues accurately while adapting their own body language to create culturally responsive therapeutic environments.

Cultural Variations in Eye Contact, Personal Space, and Touch

Eye contact, personal space, and physical touch form the foundation of nonverbal communication, but their meaning varies dramatically across cultures in ways that directly impact therapeutic relationships.

Eye Contact Patterns reflect cultural values about respect, authority, intimacy, and appropriate social interaction that influence how clients perceive therapeutic relationships.

In many Western cultures, direct eye contact signals honesty, engagement, and respect. Therapists are trained to maintain appropriate eye contact as a sign of attentiveness and connection. But this expectation can create immediate cultural conflicts with clients from cultures where direct eye contact has different meanings.

Many Asian cultures view direct eye contact with authority figures as disrespectful or challenging. Clients from these backgrounds might avoid eye contact as a sign of respect rather than avoidance. Pushing for eye contact can increase discomfort and damage the therapeutic relationship.

Some African cultures use eye contact patterns that emphasize listening versus speaking roles, where direct eye contact is appropriate when speaking but not when listening. Misunderstanding these patterns can lead to misinterpretation of engagement levels.

Many Indigenous cultures have specific eye contact protocols related to age, gender, and spiritual practices that influence appropriate therapeutic interaction patterns.

Rather than insisting on Western eye contact norms, effective MI practitioners learn to read cultural cues and adapt their expectations accordingly. You might need to interpret indirect eye contact as respect rather than avoidance while modifying your own eye contact patterns to match cultural expectations.

Personal Space Preferences vary dramatically across cultures and directly influence how comfortable clients feel in therapeutic settings.

Northern European and North American cultures typically prefer larger personal space bubbles, especially in professional settings. Clients from these backgrounds might feel crowded or invaded if you sit too close or if your office furniture arrangement doesn't provide adequate distance.

Many Latin American and Middle Eastern cultures operate with smaller personal space expectations and might interpret larger distances as coldness or rejection. Clients from these backgrounds might feel disconnected or unwelcome in sterile, distant therapeutic arrangements.

Mediterranean cultures often use closer physical proximity and more animated gestures that require different spatial considerations than cultures that emphasize restraint and controlled movement.

Some Asian cultures have complex spatial protocols that reflect social hierarchy, gender considerations, and respect patterns that influence appropriate therapeutic seating arrangements and office organization.

Understanding and accommodating these spatial preferences can significantly impact therapeutic comfort and engagement. This might mean having flexible seating arrangements, paying attention to client comfort with proximity, and adjusting your own spatial behavior to match cultural expectations.

Touch Boundaries represent perhaps the most sensitive area of cultural nonverbal communication, where misunderstanding can create serious therapeutic problems.

Many Western therapeutic traditions maintain strict no-touch boundaries that can feel cold or rejecting to clients from cultures where appropriate touch is part of supportive relationships. Handshakes, brief shoulder touches, or greeting hugs might be expected expressions of warmth and connection.

However, many cultures have strict religious or cultural prohibitions against cross-gender touch that make any physical contact inappropriate or offensive. Islamic traditions often prohibit physical contact between unrelated men and women. Orthodox Jewish culture has similar restrictions.

Some cultures have specific touch protocols related to age, status, or spiritual considerations that influence appropriate therapeutic boundaries. What feels supportive to someone from one culture might feel invasive or disrespectful to someone from another.

The key is learning to read cultural cues about touch preferences while maintaining appropriate professional boundaries. This might mean offering handshakes without assuming they'll be accepted, understanding when touch avoidance reflects cultural respect rather than personal rejection, and finding alternative ways to express warmth and support that align with cultural expectations.

Understanding Silence and Pause Patterns Across Cultures

Silence in therapeutic conversations carries different meanings across cultures, and misinterpreting these patterns can damage therapeutic relationships or miss important clinical information.

Comfortable Silence exists in some cultures where pauses in conversation represent reflection, respect, or processing time rather than awkwardness or avoidance.

Many Indigenous cultures value silence as sacred space for consideration and spiritual connection. Rushing to fill these silences can interfere with natural processing patterns and cultural communication styles.

Some Asian cultures use silence to show respect for what has been said, to consider responses carefully, or to avoid hasty statements that might cause offense or create conflict.

Certain Northern European cultures view silence as comfortable companionship rather than social failure, where sitting quietly together demonstrates ease rather than awkwardness.

Learning to tolerate and work with these culturally comfortable silences requires adjusting your own anxiety about quiet moments while learning to read whether silence represents processing, resistance, or cultural communication patterns.

Processing Time Variations affect how long clients need between questions and responses, between topics, and between sessions to integrate therapeutic conversations.

Some cultures emphasize quick, efficient communication where rapid responses demonstrate engagement and competence. Clients from these backgrounds might feel pressure to respond immediately and might interpret therapeutic patience as lack of confidence or competence.

Other cultures value careful consideration where thoughtful responses are more important than quick ones. Clients from these backgrounds might need more time to formulate responses and might feel rushed or disrespected by therapeutic pacing that doesn't accommodate reflection time.

Certain cultures have specific reflection protocols where important questions deserve extended consideration, family consultation, or spiritual reflection before responses are appropriate. Understanding these patterns prevents misinterpretation of slow responses as resistance or lack of engagement.

Respectful Pause Patterns in some cultures indicate appropriate deference to authority, consideration of what has been shared, or cultural courtesy that creates space for others to continue speaking.

These pauses might seem like incomplete thoughts or hesitation to therapists from cultures that value direct, complete expression. But interpreting them as uncertainty or resistance misses their cultural meaning and can lead to inappropriate therapeutic responses.

Learning to read these pause patterns helps you understand when clients are showing cultural respect, when they're processing information, and when they might need encouragement to continue sharing.

Facial Expressions and Emotional Display Rules

Every culture has implicit rules about appropriate emotional expression, facial display, and emotional regulation that influence how people communicate feelings and respond to others' emotions.

Emotional Restraint Cultures value controlled facial expression and emotional regulation as signs of maturity, strength, and social consideration. Clients from these backgrounds might express intense emotions through subtle facial cues that could be missed by therapists expecting more dramatic expression.

Many East Asian cultures emphasize emotional control where open expression of distress, anger, or even joy might be seen as immature or socially disruptive. Understanding these display rules prevents misinterpretation of flat affect as depression or lack of engagement.

Some Northern European cultures view emotional restraint as appropriate professional behavior and might interpret therapist emotional expressiveness as unprofessional or boundary-violating.

Certain religious cultures have specific expectations about emotional display that influence therapeutic expression and response patterns. Understanding these expectations helps you match your own emotional expression to cultural comfort levels.

Emotional Expression Cultures value open emotional communication as signs of authenticity, connection, and social engagement. Clients from these backgrounds might express feelings more dramatically and might expect reciprocal emotional responsiveness from therapists.

Many Latin American cultures encourage emotional expression as healthy communication and might interpret therapeutic emotional neutrality as coldness or lack of caring.

Some African American cultural traditions include expressive emotional communication patterns that therapists might misinterpret as excessive or inappropriate if they don't understand cultural context.

Mediterranean cultures often include animated facial expression and emotional communication that requires different therapeutic responses than cultures emphasizing restraint.

Learning to match your emotional responsiveness to cultural expectations while maintaining professional boundaries creates more comfortable therapeutic environments for clients from expressive cultural backgrounds.

Gender-Specific Display Rules in many cultures create different expectations for men and women around emotional expression that influence therapeutic engagement and goal-setting.

Traditional masculine roles in many cultures discourage emotional expression or vulnerability, making it particularly challenging for men to engage in therapeutic work that requires sharing feelings or admitting problems.

Traditional feminine roles might encourage emotional expression but discourage anger, assertiveness, or independence in ways that influence therapeutic goals and intervention strategies.

Understanding these gender-specific cultural patterns helps you work within rather than against cultural expectations while still supporting therapeutic growth and change.

Case Study: Adapting Nonverbal Communication for Cultural Responsiveness

Let me share a detailed example of how nonverbal cultural adaptation worked in practice with Yuki, a 28-year-old Japanese American woman who came to see me for social anxiety.

When Yuki first entered my office, she bowed slightly, removed her shoes (which I hadn't expected), and sat on the very edge of the chair with perfect posture, hands folded, eyes downcast. She spoke softly, paused frequently, and often covered her mouth when laughing.

Using Western therapeutic assumptions, I might have interpreted her behavior as severe social anxiety, low self-esteem, or cultural shame.

I might have encouraged her to sit back, make eye contact, and express herself more directly.

Instead, I recognized her behavior as culturally appropriate respect and courtesy. Her posture demonstrated attention and consideration. Her soft speech and downcast eyes showed appropriate deference. Her frequent pauses indicated careful thought about her responses.

Rather than trying to change her nonverbal behavior, I adapted my own to match her cultural expectations. I sat more formally, moderated my eye contact, and spoke more softly. I allowed longer pauses for her responses and avoided interpreting her restraint as pathology.

As Yuki became more comfortable, she began sharing that her social anxiety was specifically related to navigating between Japanese cultural expectations at home and American cultural expectations at work and school. She felt caught between different nonverbal communication systems that seemed to require different versions of herself.

We worked together to understand her nonverbal code-switching as a sophisticated cultural skill rather than a problem to be solved. Yuki learned to appreciate her ability to adapt to different cultural contexts while developing comfort with both her Japanese and American communication styles.

The breakthrough came when I validated her cultural communication patterns as appropriate and skilled rather than asking her to adopt Western nonverbal norms. Once she felt understood and respected, she could work on the specific social situations that created genuine anxiety while maintaining her cultural authenticity.

Six months later, Yuki reported significant improvement in her social anxiety, largely through developing pride in her bicultural communication competence rather than feeling shame about cultural differences.

Adapting MI Body Language for Cultural Responsiveness

Effective culturally responsive MI requires adapting your own nonverbal behavior to match client cultural expectations while maintaining therapeutic authenticity and professional boundaries.

Postural Adaptations involve adjusting your body position, seating arrangement, and physical presence to align with cultural expectations about appropriate professional relationships.

For clients from cultures that emphasize formal respect, maintaining more upright posture, formal seating arrangements, and professional distance might be necessary to create comfort and demonstrate appropriate boundaries.

For clients from cultures that value warmth and connection, more relaxed posture, closer seating, and informal arrangement might be needed to avoid seeming cold or rejecting.

Understanding hierarchical expectations helps you position yourself appropriately relative to client cultural expectations about authority, age, and professional relationships.

Gestural Modifications require learning which hand movements, pointing patterns, and physical expressions are appropriate or potentially offensive across different cultural contexts.

Many cultures have specific meanings for hand gestures that are neutral in Western contexts but offensive elsewhere. Learning basic gestural awareness prevents accidental cultural insults.

Some cultures emphasize controlled, minimal gesturing as professional behavior while others expect more animated expression as signs of engagement and authenticity.

Religious considerations might influence appropriate gesturing patterns, especially around spiritual topics or when working with clients who have specific religious requirements about physical expression.

Facial Expression Matching involves calibrating your emotional expressiveness to match client cultural comfort levels while maintaining therapeutic authenticity.

For clients from emotionally restrained cultures, excessive facial expressiveness might feel inappropriate or boundary-violating. Matching their level of emotional restraint while still showing appropriate concern and engagement requires careful calibration.

For clients from emotionally expressive cultures, excessive therapeutic neutrality might feel cold or disengaged. Learning to show appropriate emotional responsiveness while maintaining professional boundaries creates better therapeutic connection.

Understanding cultural meanings of facial expressions prevents misinterpretation of client emotions while helping you express therapeutic responses in culturally appropriate ways.

Working with Cultural Nonverbal Conflicts

Sometimes clients experience internal conflicts between different cultural nonverbal expectations, especially when they're navigating multiple cultural contexts in their daily lives.

Code-Switching Stress affects many multicultural individuals who must adapt their nonverbal behavior to different cultural contexts throughout their day, which can be psychologically exhausting and create identity conflicts.

Understanding and validating these adaptive challenges helps clients appreciate their cultural competence while addressing the stress that comes from constant nonverbal code-switching.

Intergenerational Conflicts emerge when different generations within the same family have different nonverbal expectations based on acculturation, age, or cultural adaptation experiences.

These conflicts might affect family communication patterns, therapeutic engagement, and change processes in ways that require sensitive navigation of different cultural expectations within the same family system.

Professional versus Cultural Conflicts occur when workplace or educational environments require nonverbal behavior that conflicts with cultural values or family expectations about appropriate communication patterns.

Working with these conflicts requires helping clients develop strategies for navigating different cultural expectations while maintaining authentic cultural identity and family relationships.

Training Your Cultural Nonverbal Awareness

Developing cultural competence in nonverbal communication requires ongoing attention to your own cultural assumptions and active learning about different cultural communication patterns.

Self-Assessment of your own cultural nonverbal patterns helps you understand how your cultural background influences your interpretation of client behavior and your own therapeutic presentation.

What do you assume about appropriate eye contact, personal space, and emotional expression? How do your cultural patterns influence what you notice and how you interpret client nonverbal behavior?

Cultural Observation Skills involve learning to notice and interpret nonverbal cues within cultural context rather than applying universal assumptions about meaning and appropriateness.

This requires suspending judgment about client nonverbal behavior while gathering information about cultural meanings and expectations that influence therapeutic interaction patterns.

Flexible Response Development helps you adjust your own nonverbal behavior to match cultural expectations while maintaining therapeutic effectiveness and professional boundaries.

This doesn't mean mimicking client behavior but rather finding authentic ways to show respect and create comfort within different cultural frameworks.

Technology Considerations for Nonverbal Communication

Video therapy and remote sessions create additional challenges for reading and adapting to cultural nonverbal communication patterns that require specific technological considerations.

Camera Positioning affects how nonverbal cues are transmitted and interpreted across video platforms, potentially distorting or missing important cultural communication patterns.

Understanding how technology mediates nonverbal communication helps you adjust video setups to maximize cultural information while accommodating different cultural comfort levels with technology and video interaction.

Screen Distance considerations affect perceived personal space and intimacy levels across video connections, which might need adjustment based on cultural preferences for professional distance or connection.

Cultural Technology Comfort varies across different populations, and some clients might feel more comfortable with phone-only sessions that eliminate video-mediated nonverbal pressure while others might need video connection to feel appropriately engaged.

What This Means for Your Practice

Developing cultural competence in nonverbal communication requires ongoing attention to how your own cultural background influences therapeutic interaction while learning to read and adapt to diverse cultural communication patterns.

Cultural Humility about nonverbal communication means approaching each client as a teacher about their cultural communication patterns while remaining flexible in your own therapeutic presentation.

Observational Skills help you notice and interpret nonverbal cues within cultural context rather than applying universal assumptions about meaning and engagement levels.

Adaptive Responsiveness involves adjusting your own nonverbal behavior to create culturally comfortable therapeutic environments while maintaining professional authenticity and boundaries.

Ongoing Education about different cultural nonverbal patterns prevents assumptions and misinterpretations that could damage therapeutic relationships or miss important clinical information.

Most importantly, approach nonverbal communication as cultural conversation rather than universal language. What feels natural and appropriate to you might feel foreign or uncomfortable to clients from different cultural backgrounds, and what seems unusual to you might be perfectly appropriate cultural communication.

When you can read and adapt to different cultural nonverbal patterns while maintaining MI's collaborative spirit, you create therapeutic relationships that feel culturally familiar and respectful rather than foreign or demanding. That's not just good cultural competence—it's effective therapy that honors the whole person within their cultural communication framework.

Building Your Nonverbal Cultural Repertoire

Effective cultural responsiveness in nonverbal communication requires building a flexible repertoire of therapeutic presentations that can adapt to diverse cultural expectations without losing authenticity or effectiveness.

This isn't about becoming a cultural chameleon or abandoning your own authentic style. It's about developing the cultural flexibility to create comfortable therapeutic environments for clients from different backgrounds while maintaining your professional effectiveness and personal integrity.

Start by examining your own cultural assumptions about appropriate nonverbal behavior. Then begin paying attention to how clients from different backgrounds communicate nonverbally, asking questions when you're unsure about cultural meanings rather than making assumptions.

Most importantly, approach each client as an individual expert in their own cultural communication patterns while offering professional support that honors rather than conflicts with their cultural nonverbal frameworks. That's culturally responsive therapy that supports both therapeutic goals and cultural authenticity.

Chapter 11: Working with Interpreters

Maintaining MI Spirit Through Translation

When Maria first walked into my office with her daughter serving as interpreter, I thought I was prepared for the complexity of trilingual therapy. I spoke some Spanish, Maria spoke limited English, and her 16-year-old daughter Carmen was fluent in both languages plus the unspoken language of family dynamics.

What I wasn't prepared for was how MI's collaborative, client-centered approach would get lost in translation—literally. Carmen would ask her mother a question, listen to a lengthy Spanish response, then turn to me and say, "She says she's fine." When I tried to reflect what seemed like complex emotions, Carmen would translate my reflection into a brief Spanish phrase that clearly missed the nuance I was attempting to convey.

After three sessions of frustration, I realized that working effectively with interpreters in MI requires much more than language conversion. It requires cultural mediation, relationship management, and careful attention to how therapeutic intentions translate across not just languages but worldviews, family dynamics, and cultural frameworks.

The interpreter becomes a crucial third person in the therapeutic relationship who can either facilitate or interfere with MI's collaborative spirit depending on their training, cultural competence, and understanding of therapeutic goals.

Selecting and Training Culturally Competent Interpreters

The most important decision you'll make about interpreter-mediated MI is choosing interpreters who understand both linguistic and cultural translation while grasping the collaborative nature of MI approaches.

Professional versus Family Interpreters presents the first major choice that affects everything else about the therapeutic process.

Professional interpreters bring language skills, ethical training, and emotional distance that can facilitate therapeutic work while maintaining appropriate boundaries. They're trained to interpret accurately without adding their own opinions or emotional reactions.

However, professional interpreters might not understand the nuances of MI approaches, might interpret too literally without conveying emotional undertones, or might not grasp the cultural context that influences both client communication and therapeutic effectiveness.

Family member interpreters bring cultural knowledge, emotional investment, and understanding of family dynamics that can enhance therapeutic understanding. They know the client's communication patterns, cultural references, and personal history in ways that professional interpreters cannot.

But family interpreters also bring their own agenda, emotional reactions, and family role expectations that can interfere with therapeutic work. They might filter information to protect family members, add their own interpretations, or become unwitting therapists themselves.

The choice depends on client preference, availability, therapeutic goals, and the specific family dynamics involved. Sometimes professional interpreters work better for sensitive topics while family interpreters facilitate cultural understanding and engagement.

Cultural Competence Beyond Language becomes crucial for effective MI interpretation because therapeutic concepts don't always translate directly across cultural frameworks.

Interpreters need to understand cultural concepts like *personalismo* in Latino cultures, concepts of face and shame in Asian cultures, or spiritual frameworks in indigenous communities that influence how therapeutic ideas are expressed and understood.

They also need to understand cultural communication patterns like indirect expression, hierarchical respect, or collective decision-making that influence how clients respond to MI techniques and how therapeutic concepts should be conveyed.

MI-Specific Training for interpreters helps them understand the collaborative, client-centered approach that differs from medical interpretation where accuracy and brevity are prioritized over therapeutic relationship-building.

MI interpreters need to understand how to convey empathic reflections, how to maintain the spirit of open-ended questions, and how to preserve the client's own words and meanings rather than summarizing or paraphrasing.

They also need to understand how to maintain therapeutic pacing, how to convey emotional undertones, and how to support rather than direct therapeutic conversations.

Pre-Session Preparation and Post-Session Debriefing

Effective interpreter-mediated MI requires systematic preparation and debriefing that ensures therapeutic intentions translate accurately while maintaining cultural responsiveness and therapeutic effectiveness.

Pre-Session Briefing should cover therapeutic goals, cultural considerations, client background, and specific MI techniques you plan to use during the session.

Explain the collaborative nature of MI, the importance of preserving client language and emotional expression, and how the interpreter's role differs from other types of interpretation they might be familiar with.

Discuss any cultural dynamics that might influence the session, specific family or community issues that could affect interpretation, and any sensitive topics that require particular cultural awareness.

Review the client's preferred terms for discussing problems, their cultural background, and any previous interpretation challenges that need attention during the upcoming session.

Role Clarification helps interpreters understand their function in MI sessions while maintaining appropriate boundaries and therapeutic focus.

Interpreters should understand that they're facilitating communication rather than providing therapy, that they should preserve client language and expression rather than summarizing, and that they should interpret therapeutic techniques rather than modifying them.

They also need to understand when to ask for clarification, how to handle cultural concepts that don't translate directly, and how to maintain neutrality while still conveying emotional undertones.

Post-Session Debriefing provides opportunities to understand cultural dynamics that influenced the session, interpretation challenges that emerged, and ways to improve future sessions.

Discuss what cultural information emerged that might influence future therapeutic work, what interpretation challenges arose that need different approaches, and what therapeutic techniques worked well or poorly in translation.

Use debriefing to educate yourself about cultural dynamics you might have missed, to improve your interpreter collaboration skills, and to plan modifications for future sessions based on what you learned.

Managing the Triadic Relationship in MI

Working with interpreters creates a three-way relationship that requires careful management to maintain MI's client-centered focus while utilizing interpreter expertise effectively.

Seating Arrangements affect power dynamics, communication flow, and cultural comfort in ways that require careful consideration.

Some clients prefer interpreters to sit between them and the therapist as cultural mediators and advocates. Others prefer interpreters to the side to maintain direct connection with the therapist while receiving language support.

Cultural hierarchies might influence seating preferences, with some clients feeling more comfortable when interpreters occupy specific positions that reflect appropriate respect patterns or family dynamics.

Experiment with different arrangements while paying attention to client comfort and communication effectiveness rather than assuming one arrangement works for all cultural contexts.

Eye Contact and Direct Address patterns need adjustment to maintain therapeutic connection while working through interpreters.

Generally, maintain eye contact with clients while speaking to them directly rather than addressing interpreters as intermediaries. This preserves the therapeutic relationship and shows respect for client agency and authority.

However, some cultural patterns might require modified eye contact approaches based on cultural respect patterns, age hierarchies, or gender considerations that influence appropriate therapeutic interaction.

Pace and Flow Management becomes more complex when every communication requires interpretation time, cultural consideration, and potential clarification.

Allow extra time for interpretation while maintaining therapeutic momentum and connection. Avoid rushing interpretation or becoming impatient with the additional time required for cultural and linguistic translation.

Build in pauses for interpretation while maintaining emotional connection and therapeutic timing that supports rather than interferes with MI's collaborative pace.

Case Study: Navigating Complex Family Dynamics Through Interpretation

Let me share a detailed example of how these dynamics played out with the Nguyen family. Mrs. Nguyen, a 45-year-old Vietnamese American woman, came to therapy for depression following her husband's death. Her 22-year-old son Duc served as interpreter.

The family dynamics were immediately complex. Mrs. Nguyen spoke limited English but understood more than she felt comfortable expressing. Duc was fluent in both languages but carried his own grief about his father's death plus responsibility for family decisions since becoming the male head of household.

In early sessions, Duc would translate his mother's emotional expressions into matter-of-fact English summaries that missed the depth of her grief. When I tried to reflect her emotions, he would translate my reflections into practical advice rather than empathic understanding.

I realized that Duc was protecting both his mother and himself from the intensity of grief while trying to present their family as strong and capable rather than struggling and needy.

Rather than challenging his protective translation, I worked with the family dynamics by acknowledging Duc's difficult position as both interpreter and family caregiver while creating space for his mother's authentic expression.

I began speaking directly to Mrs. Nguyen while asking Duc to translate my words exactly rather than summarizing them. I used simpler language that translated more directly while still conveying empathy and respect.

I also acknowledged Duc's own losses and stress while clarifying that his role was interpreter rather than family spokesperson. This allowed him to step back from the protective position while still supporting his mother.

As Mrs. Nguyen felt safer expressing her grief and Duc felt less responsible for managing her emotions, the therapeutic relationship became more authentic and effective. Mrs. Nguyen began sharing cultural aspects of her grief process that helped me understand her experience better.

The breakthrough came when I learned enough basic Vietnamese phrases to show respect for their cultural background while relying on Duc for complex interpretation. This demonstrated cultural investment while maintaining therapeutic effectiveness.

Six months later, Mrs. Nguyen was participating more actively in her community and had developed English-language support relationships while maintaining her cultural identity and family connections.

Cultural Nuance in Therapeutic Translation

Effective MI interpretation requires understanding how therapeutic concepts translate not just linguistically but culturally, ensuring that MI's collaborative spirit survives the translation process.

Emotional Vocabulary Translation becomes complex when languages have different emotional concepts or when cultural display rules influence how emotions are expressed and interpreted.

Some languages have emotional terms that don't exist in English, requiring interpreters to explain cultural concepts rather than simply translating words. Other languages might not distinguish between emotions that are separate in English.

Cultural emotional display rules influence how feelings are appropriately expressed, which might require interpreters to explain cultural context rather than just translating emotional content.

Metaphor and Imagery Translation requires cultural knowledge about symbolic meanings, religious references, and cultural imagery that carry therapeutic significance beyond literal translation.

Cultural metaphors for healing, change, strength, or spiritual concepts might not translate directly but carry important meaning for understanding client worldviews and therapeutic resources.

Religious or spiritual imagery might require cultural explanation to preserve therapeutic significance while avoiding cultural misinterpretation or appropriation.

Authority and Relationship Language varies significantly across cultures in ways that influence how therapeutic relationships are understood and how change processes are conceptualized.

Some cultures have specific language for authority relationships that might influence how clients understand therapeutic roles and expectations about change processes.

Family relationship language might carry cultural expectations about decision-making, support, and change processes that affect therapeutic goals and intervention strategies.

Working with Professional Interpretation Services

When family interpreters aren't appropriate or available, working with professional interpretation services requires specific preparation and collaboration strategies.

Service Selection Criteria should include cultural competence, mental health experience, and understanding of therapeutic versus medical interpretation requirements.

Medical interpreters are trained for accuracy and brevity, which might not serve MI's relationship-building and emotional processing goals. Therapeutic interpreters need training in mental health concepts and collaborative communication approaches.

Cultural matching might be important for sensitive topics or when cultural knowledge significantly influences therapeutic understanding and intervention effectiveness.

Remote Interpretation Considerations create additional challenges for maintaining therapeutic connection while utilizing professional interpretation services.

Video interpretation allows for nonverbal communication and cultural cues that phone interpretation might miss, but it also creates technological barriers and reduced intimacy that might affect therapeutic relationships.

Phone interpretation eliminates nonverbal cultural information while potentially feeling less personal or connected than in-person interpretation services.

Confidentiality and Ethics require clear agreements about professional boundaries, confidentiality maintenance, and appropriate interpreter roles in therapeutic relationships.

Professional interpreters need to understand therapeutic confidentiality requirements while maintaining appropriate boundaries about their role in ongoing therapeutic relationships.

Technology Considerations for Remote Interpretation

Technology-mediated interpretation creates additional complexity for maintaining MI's collaborative spirit while managing technical, cultural, and therapeutic challenges.

Platform Selection affects interpretation quality, cultural connection, and therapeutic effectiveness in ways that require careful consideration of client needs and preferences.

Some clients might prefer phone interpretation for privacy reasons while others need video connection for cultural and therapeutic connection.

Technology comfort varies across cultural and generational lines, requiring assessment of client preferences and technological capabilities before selecting interpretation platforms.

Audio Quality and Timing become crucial for accurate interpretation and therapeutic connection when technology mediates both therapeutic and interpretation relationships.

Poor audio quality can interfere with both interpretation accuracy and emotional connection, requiring backup plans and technical preparation for effective sessions.

Timing delays can disrupt therapeutic pacing and emotional connection, requiring adjustment of MI techniques to accommodate technological limitations.

Cultural Technology Comfort varies across different populations, with some clients preferring in-person interpretation while others appreciate technology-mediated options for privacy or accessibility reasons.

Interpreter Ethics and Boundary Management

Working with interpreters requires clear understanding of ethical responsibilities, professional boundaries, and role expectations that maintain therapeutic effectiveness while protecting all parties involved.

Confidentiality Requirements extend to interpreters who become privy to sensitive personal information while facilitating therapeutic communication.

Professional interpreters should have clear confidentiality training and agreements while family interpreters might need education about privacy expectations and appropriate information sharing.

Cultural Advocacy versus Neutrality creates tension when interpreters observe cultural misunderstandings or potentially harmful therapeutic approaches that conflict with client cultural values.

Interpreters need guidelines about when and how to provide cultural information that enhances therapeutic understanding without overstepping appropriate professional boundaries.

Dual Relationship Challenges emerge when family member interpreters have their own therapeutic needs or when professional interpreters develop ongoing relationships with clients outside of therapeutic contexts.

Clear role boundaries help prevent confusion about therapeutic versus interpretation relationships while maintaining appropriate professional standards.

Training Implications for Therapists

Effective interpreter-mediated MI requires specific skills and knowledge that should be included in professional training and continuing education for therapists working in diverse communities.

Interpreter Collaboration Skills include communication strategies, cultural awareness, and relationship management techniques that maximize interpretation effectiveness while maintaining therapeutic goals.

Cultural Assessment Through Interpretation requires understanding how to gather cultural information when direct communication is limited and how to assess therapeutic progress when cultural and linguistic barriers exist.

Modified MI Techniques for interpreter-mediated sessions might include adjusted pacing, simplified language, and alternative strategies that maintain therapeutic effectiveness while accommodating interpretation requirements.

What This Means for Your Practice

Working effectively with interpreters in MI requires systematic preparation, cultural awareness, and relationship management skills that enhance rather than complicate therapeutic work.

Interpreter Selection should prioritize cultural competence and MI understanding over just language skills, while considering client preferences and therapeutic goals in making interpretation decisions.

Systematic Preparation ensures that interpreters understand therapeutic goals, cultural considerations, and their specific role in facilitating rather than directing therapeutic conversations.

Relationship Management maintains client-centered focus while utilizing interpreter expertise effectively and managing the complex dynamics that emerge in triadic therapeutic relationships.

Cultural Learning treats interpretation sessions as opportunities for cultural education that enhances your ability to work effectively with clients from different backgrounds.

Quality Monitoring involves ongoing assessment of interpretation effectiveness, cultural responsiveness, and therapeutic outcomes that inform improvements in interpreter collaboration.

Most importantly, approach interpreter-mediated MI as collaborative cultural work that can enhance rather than complicate therapeutic relationships when managed skillfully and respectfully.

When you can work effectively with interpreters while maintaining MI's collaborative spirit, you create therapeutic opportunities for clients who might otherwise lack access to culturally responsive mental health services. That's not just good clinical practice—it's social justice work that ensures MI's benefits are available across linguistic and cultural communities.

Chapter 12: Family-Centered MI

When Individual Autonomy Isn't Primary?

When I first started seeing the Rodriguez family for their teenage son Miguel's substance use, I made the classic mistake of trying to separate individual from family issues. I wanted to work with Miguel alone, believing that family involvement would compromise his autonomy and my ability to build therapeutic rapport with him.

But Miguel kept talking about his family in every session. His concerns about disappointing his parents, his worry about his younger siblings looking up to him, his pride in being the first in his family to attend college—these weren't obstacles to individual therapy. They were the core motivations that could drive his recovery.

Mrs. Rodriguez called me after the third session. "Doctor, I don't understand why you won't talk to us. Miguel is our son, and his problems affect our whole family. How can you help him if you don't understand us?"

She was right. In Latino culture, Miguel's substance use wasn't an individual problem requiring individual solutions. It was a family concern requiring family involvement, family resources, and family-supported change. My Western therapeutic assumptions about individual autonomy were actually interfering with the collectivist approaches that felt natural and effective for this family.

That's when I realized that MI can be even more powerful when it works within family systems rather than trying to extract individuals from their cultural and familial contexts.

Identifying Appropriate Family Members for Inclusion

The first challenge in family-centered MI involves understanding who constitutes "family" in different cultural contexts and which family members should be included in therapeutic conversations.

Extended Family Considerations go beyond nuclear family to include grandparents, aunts, uncles, and other relatives who might play crucial roles in decision-making, support provision, and cultural guidance.

In many cultures, grandparents hold special authority and wisdom that influence major family decisions. Including them in MI conversations might be essential for sustainable change, especially when their support or approval affects family dynamics.

Godparents, family friends, or community members might function as family and could provide important support or influence that affects therapeutic outcomes.

The key is asking clients about their family definition rather than assuming nuclear family models apply across all cultural contexts.

Decision-Making Authority patterns help you understand which family members need to be involved for decisions to feel legitimate and sustainable within the family system.

Some cultures give primary decision-making authority to fathers or male elders, while others operate through consensus among all adult family members. Understanding these patterns helps you include appropriate people in therapeutic planning.

Age-based authority systems might require elder involvement for major decisions, while education-based systems might defer to family members with professional or educational credentials.

Cultural Role Identification helps you understand which family members serve specific functions that could support or complicate therapeutic goals.

Family peacemakers might be crucial for managing conflicts that arise during change processes. Family historians might provide cultural wisdom and context that support motivation and planning.

Family advocates might serve as bridges between individual needs and collective concerns, while family protectors might need reassurance about therapeutic goals before they support individual change efforts.

Family Hierarchy Navigation requires understanding and respecting appropriate roles, communication patterns, and decision-making processes that maintain family harmony while supporting therapeutic goals.

This doesn't mean accepting unhealthy family dynamics, but it does mean working within existing family structures while creating opportunities for healthy change that feels culturally appropriate and sustainable.

Facilitating Family MI Conversations

Conducting MI with multiple family members requires modified techniques that maintain the collaborative spirit while managing complex group dynamics, competing perspectives, and cultural considerations.

Opening Family Sessions need to establish safety, clarify roles, and create structure that allows everyone to participate while maintaining therapeutic focus.

Begin by acknowledging everyone present and their relationship to the primary client, showing respect for their investment in the family member's well-being while clarifying therapeutic goals.

Explain how family MI differs from individual therapy, emphasizing that everyone's perspective matters while maintaining focus on supporting the identified client's change process.

Establish ground rules about respect, confidentiality, and communication that honor cultural patterns while creating space for honest conversation about change.

Managing Multiple Perspectives requires balancing different family members' viewpoints while maintaining focus on the client's own motivation and goals.

Use reflective listening to acknowledge each family member's concerns while connecting their perspectives to the client's well-being and change process.

Look for common ground among different family viewpoints that can support unified family approaches to change while respecting individual differences.

Avoid taking sides in family conflicts while helping family members understand how their different perspectives might actually complement each other in supporting change.

Cultural Communication Adaptation ensures that therapeutic techniques work within existing family communication patterns rather than imposing Western family therapy models.

Some families communicate through hierarchy where certain members speak first or have final authority. Working within these patterns while creating space for everyone's input requires cultural sensitivity and flexibility.

Other families use indirect communication or storytelling approaches that might seem inefficient but actually convey important information and cultural wisdom.

Emotional expression patterns vary dramatically across cultures, with some families encouraging open expression while others prefer more controlled communication styles.

Case Study: Family-Centered Approach to Substance Use Recovery

The Chen family came to see me when their 19-year-old son David was arrested for DUI. The family included David's parents, both professionals who had immigrated from Taiwan twenty years earlier, and his 16-year-old sister Amy.

The family was deeply concerned about bringing shame to their family name and community reputation. They were also confused about American approaches to addiction treatment and worried that professional intervention might make things worse.

Using individual MI approaches, I might have focused on David's personal motivation for change while viewing family concerns as external pressure that could interfere with authentic change commitment.

Instead, I worked with the family's collectivist values by exploring how David's recovery could honor family values while addressing everyone's concerns about his drinking.

I started by acknowledging the family's love for David and their commitment to his success, framing their involvement as strength rather than interference. I then explored how David's drinking affected each family member and what recovery would mean for the whole family.

David initially minimized his drinking and seemed resistant to change when the focus was on individual consequences. But when we explored how his drinking affected his parents' stress levels and his sister's worries about him, he became much more engaged.

The breakthrough came when we connected David's recovery to his goals of becoming a role model for Amy and honoring his parents' sacrifices in immigrating to provide opportunities for their children.

David's motivation for change became much stronger when it was connected to family values and relationships rather than individual consequences or health concerns that felt abstract to him.

We worked together to develop family-supported recovery strategies. His parents agreed to cultural approaches like increased family time and community involvement while learning about American addiction treatment resources.

Amy became David's accountability partner and supporter, while David took responsibility for demonstrating recovery commitment through actions rather than just words.

Six months later, David was sober and actively involved in cultural community activities that provided both family connection and peer support for his recovery. The family felt closer and more unified through the process rather than fragmented by individual treatment approaches.

Navigating Conflicting Family Perspectives on Change

Family members often have different opinions about problems, solutions, and change goals that require careful navigation to maintain therapeutic focus while honoring legitimate concerns.

Competing Problem Definitions emerge when family members disagree about the nature of the problem, its severity, or its causes, requiring therapeutic approaches that acknowledge different perspectives while maintaining focus on change.

Parents might view substance use as moral failure requiring discipline and control while young adults see it as experimentation requiring understanding and support. Working with these different definitions without taking sides requires skillful therapeutic navigation.

Cultural versus medical explanations for mental health problems might create family conflicts about appropriate treatment approaches that require integration rather than choosing sides.

Different Change Goals within families require exploration of how different family members' goals might actually complement each other while supporting the client's authentic change process.

Parents might want complete abstinence while clients prefer moderation goals. Finding common ground around harm reduction and health improvement can bridge these differences while supporting sustainable change.

Academic versus social goals might seem conflicting but could actually support each other when integrated thoughtfully into comprehensive change planning.

Resource and Support Disagreements affect how families approach change implementation and what kinds of support feel helpful versus intrusive.

Some family members might want professional treatment while others prefer family-based solutions. Exploring how different approaches might complement each other creates comprehensive support systems.

Financial resources, time availability, and family priorities require negotiation that honors everyone's constraints while maximizing support for change processes.

Maintaining Client Confidentiality Within Family Systems

Family-centered MI requires careful navigation of confidentiality requirements while honoring family involvement and cultural expectations about information sharing.

Individual versus Family Confidentiality creates complex ethical terrain when family members expect information sharing that might conflict with individual confidentiality requirements.

Clarifying confidentiality boundaries early in family work prevents misunderstandings while helping families understand professional requirements and appropriate information sharing patterns.

Some information might be appropriate for family sharing while other information requires individual confidentiality, requiring ongoing negotiation and clear communication about boundaries.

Cultural Information Sharing Expectations might conflict with Western confidentiality requirements, creating tension that requires careful cultural navigation and explanation.

Some cultures expect family leaders to have access to all information affecting family members, while professional ethics require individual consent for information sharing.

Working with these cultural expectations while maintaining ethical requirements requires education, negotiation, and sometimes cultural mediation to find approaches that honor both cultural values and professional standards.

Safety Considerations might require information sharing that goes beyond normal confidentiality requirements when family dynamics create safety risks or when change processes affect family safety.

Substance use, domestic violence, or self-harm risks might require family communication that exceeds normal confidentiality boundaries while still respecting individual autonomy and cultural values.

Adapting MI Techniques for Family Contexts

Standard MI techniques require modification to work effectively with multiple family members while maintaining the collaborative spirit that makes MI effective across individual and family contexts.

Reflective Listening with Multiple Speakers requires skills for managing complex communication patterns while ensuring everyone feels heard and understood.

Reflect individual family members' perspectives while also reflecting family themes and common concerns that connect different viewpoints around shared values and goals.

Use reflective listening to manage family conflicts by acknowledging different perspectives without taking sides while helping family members understand each other's concerns.

Open-Ended Questions for Family Exploration can uncover family strengths, values, and resources that support individual change while strengthening family relationships.

"What kind of family do you want to be?" explores collective identity and values that can motivate both individual change and family growth.

"How do you think your ancestors would want you to handle this challenge?" connects current problems to cultural wisdom and family legacy that provide motivation and guidance.

Family-Focused Affirmations recognize both individual strengths and family resources that support change while honoring cultural values and family identity.

"Your family's commitment to each other is really clear" affirms family bonds that can support individual change while strengthening family cohesion.

"It's obvious that you all want what's best for [client name]" validates family investment while redirecting energy toward supportive rather than controlling approaches.

Family Change Summaries weave together individual motivation, family concerns, and collective goals in ways that support both personal autonomy and family harmony.

"[Client] wants to make this change for their own health and happiness, but also because they love this family and want to honor the values you've all worked to maintain. And everyone here wants to support [client] while also taking care of the whole family."

Working with Family Resistance and Ambivalence

Family members might have their own ambivalence about change that affects their support for individual change efforts, requiring therapeutic attention to family-level motivation and change processes.

Family Investment in Status Quo might create resistance when individual changes threaten family roles, dynamics, or cultural expectations that provide stability and predictability.

Family members might fear that individual change will disrupt family harmony, challenge traditional roles, or create distance between family members who have been closely connected.

Understanding and addressing these fears while supporting healthy change requires helping families envision how individual growth can strengthen rather than threaten family relationships.

Cultural Change Anxiety emerges when individual changes seem to threaten cultural identity, traditional values, or family connection to cultural community and practices.

Families might worry that therapy or individual change efforts will lead to cultural assimilation that disconnects family members from cultural roots and community belonging.

Working with these concerns requires demonstrating how individual change can honor rather than abandon cultural values while supporting healthy family functioning within cultural contexts.

Intergenerational Conflicts about change goals, methods, and pace require navigation that honors both traditional wisdom and contemporary needs while supporting family unity.

Older generations might prefer traditional approaches while younger generations favor contemporary methods, creating family tensions that affect individual change support.

Finding ways to integrate traditional and contemporary approaches often resolves these conflicts while strengthening rather than dividing family relationships.

Building on Family Strengths and Resources

Every family system has strengths, resources, and wisdom that can support individual change when identified and activated through skillful family-centered MI.

Cultural Family Traditions often include approaches to problem-solving, mutual support, and change processes that can complement professional therapeutic interventions.

Family storytelling traditions might provide frameworks for understanding problems and change that feel more natural than clinical approaches while still supporting therapeutic goals.

Religious or spiritual family practices might offer resources for motivation, support, and change processes that strengthen rather than compete with therapeutic work.

Family Network Resources extend beyond immediate family to include extended family, community connections, and cultural resources that can provide practical and emotional support for change efforts.

Grandparents, aunts, uncles, and family friends might offer different types of support that complement therapeutic work while providing cultural grounding and community connection.

Community leaders, religious figures, or cultural mentors might provide guidance and support that reinforces therapeutic goals while maintaining cultural authenticity and community belonging.

Family Resilience History includes previous experiences of successfully handling challenges that can provide models and confidence for addressing current problems.

"How has your family gotten through difficult times before?" identifies family coping strategies and resources that can support current change efforts.

"What strengths has your family always had that might help with this challenge?" connects current problems to existing family resources and cultural strengths.

Technology Considerations for Family MI Sessions

Video technology creates additional challenges for managing family MI sessions while maintaining therapeutic effectiveness and family engagement across multiple participants.

Screen Management for multiple family members requires technical setup that allows everyone to participate effectively while maintaining therapeutic connection and family dynamics.

Large family sessions might require multiple devices or screen arrangements that accommodate different family members' technology comfort and availability.

Cultural Technology Comfort varies across family members and generations, requiring flexible approaches that accommodate different comfort levels while maintaining family inclusion and therapeutic effectiveness.

Some family members might prefer phone participation while others need video connection, requiring hybrid approaches that accommodate different preferences and technological capabilities.

Family Privacy Considerations become more complex when family members participate from different locations or when family sessions include sensitive topics that require secure communication platforms.

Training Implications for Family-Centered MI

Effective family-centered MI requires additional skills and knowledge beyond individual MI training that should be included in professional development for therapists working with diverse families.

Family Systems Understanding provides foundation for understanding how individual problems develop and persist within family contexts while identifying family resources that can support individual change.

Cultural Family Variation education helps therapists understand how different cultures organize family life, decision-making, and support systems that influence therapeutic approaches and intervention effectiveness.

Group Process Management skills help therapists manage complex family dynamics while maintaining therapeutic focus and ensuring that all family members feel heard and valued.

What This Means for Your Practice

Family-centered MI requires fundamental shifts in therapeutic thinking that move beyond individual focus to systems approaches that honor cultural values while supporting individual change within family contexts.

Cultural Family Assessment becomes crucial for understanding who constitutes family, how families make decisions, and what family involvement looks like across different cultural contexts.

Inclusive Planning involves family members in therapeutic goal-setting and change planning in ways that honor individual autonomy while utilizing family support and cultural resources.

Ethical Navigation requires balancing individual confidentiality with family involvement expectations while maintaining cultural sensitivity and professional boundaries.

Skills Development includes group facilitation, family communication management, and cultural navigation abilities that enhance individual MI skills while adding family systems competencies.

Most importantly, approach family-centered MI as cultural practice that honors collective values while supporting individual change within contexts that provide meaning, support, and cultural authenticity.

When you can work skillfully with families while maintaining MI's collaborative spirit, you create therapeutic opportunities that feel culturally natural while providing professional resources that enhance rather than compete with family strengths and cultural wisdom. That's not just good family therapy—it's culturally responsive practice that supports both individual change and family resilience.

Chapter 13: Incorporating Faith into Change Conversations

When Father Miguel came to see me about his drinking problem, he brought more than just personal struggles with alcohol. He brought his Catholic faith, his community responsibilities, his sense of calling to serve others, and his profound shame about not living up to the spiritual standards he preached to his congregation.

"How can I tell people about God's love and forgiveness when I can't forgive myself?" he asked during our first session. "How can I lead others spiritually when I feel so lost myself?"

Father Miguel's question cut to the heart of a crucial therapeutic challenge: How do you integrate spiritual resources into MI when clients' faith is simultaneously a source of strength and a source of conflict? How do you work with religious frameworks that might view addiction as sin while supporting change approaches that emphasize self-compassion and realistic goal-setting?

Traditional MI often treats spirituality as peripheral to change processes, something to be acknowledged respectfully but not central to therapeutic work. But for many clients, faith isn't optional—it's the lens through which they understand their problems, their possibilities, and their identity.

This means effective MI with spiritual clients requires understanding religious frameworks, collaborating with faith communities, and finding ways to enhance rather than compete with spiritual resources that can support lasting change.

Assessment of Spiritual Resources and Barriers

Before integrating spiritual elements into MI, you need to understand how faith functions in your client's life—where it provides resources and where it might create barriers to change.

Religious Identity Exploration goes beyond denominational affiliation to understand how faith shapes identity, values, decision-making, and approaches to problems and change.

Some clients have deep, integrated faith that influences every aspect of their lives while others have complicated relationships with religion that include both positive resources and negative associations.

Cultural versus personal religion creates additional complexity when clients feel connected to cultural religious traditions while questioning personal beliefs or when family religious expectations conflict with individual spiritual experiences.

"What role does faith play in your daily life?" opens exploration of religious resources without making assumptions about belief levels or religious commitment.

"How do your spiritual beliefs help you understand what you're going through?" identifies religious frameworks that influence problem interpretation and change motivation.

Spiritual Coping Assessment reveals how clients use religious resources to manage stress, find meaning, and maintain hope during difficult periods.

Positive religious coping might include prayer, meditation, scripture reading, community worship, or seeking guidance from religious leaders that provide comfort and strength during challenges.

Negative religious coping might include spiritual struggles, religious guilt, feeling abandoned by God, or viewing problems as divine punishment that interfere with healing and change.

Understanding both positive and negative spiritual coping patterns helps you support helpful religious resources while addressing spiritual barriers that might interfere with change processes.

Community Faith Resources include relationships with religious leaders, faith community support, and spiritual practices that can complement professional therapeutic services.

Active religious communities often provide practical support, emotional encouragement, and spiritual guidance that can significantly enhance therapeutic outcomes when integrated appropriately.

Religious leaders might offer pastoral care, spiritual direction, or community resources that support change goals while providing cultural and spiritual grounding that professional therapy cannot provide.

Spiritual Barriers to Change

Faith can sometimes create obstacles to change when religious beliefs conflict with therapeutic approaches or when spiritual guilt and shame interfere with self-compassion and realistic goal-setting.

Religious Guilt and Shame often complicate mental health and addiction recovery when clients view their problems as moral failures rather than health conditions requiring treatment and support.

"Good Christians don't get depressed" or "People with strong faith don't need professional help" create spiritual barriers that prevent help-seeking while increasing self-criticism and shame.

Religious perfectionism might set unrealistic standards for change that create failure cycles and spiritual discouragement when clients can't meet impossible religious expectations.

Working with religious guilt requires helping clients find theological resources for self-compassion, forgiveness, and realistic approaches to change that align with rather than conflict with spiritual values.

Theological Conflicts with therapeutic approaches might create tension when religious beliefs about personal responsibility, divine intervention, or moral behavior seem to conflict with evidence-based treatment approaches.

Some religious traditions emphasize willpower and moral choice in ways that might conflict with disease models of addiction or medical approaches to mental health treatment.

Faith healing beliefs might compete with professional treatment approaches, creating tension about whether seeking professional help demonstrates insufficient faith or spiritual failure.

These conflicts don't require choosing between faith and professional help, but they do require careful integration that honors both spiritual beliefs and effective treatment approaches.

Community Religious Pressure might create additional barriers when faith communities have stigmatizing attitudes toward mental health problems or when seeking professional help violates cultural religious expectations.

Some religious communities might view mental health struggles as spiritual weakness or inadequate faith that create shame and isolation for individuals needing professional support.

Family religious expectations might discourage professional help-seeking while expecting faith-based solutions that might not be sufficient for complex mental health or addiction problems.

Working with community religious pressure requires understanding cultural religious contexts while helping clients navigate between spiritual community expectations and personal health needs.

Case Study: Integrating Islamic Faith with Addiction Recovery

Amira was a 32-year-old Muslim woman who came to see me for help with prescription pain medication dependence that had developed following surgery for a chronic pain condition. Her faith was central to her identity, but she felt it was complicating rather than supporting her recovery efforts.

Amira felt profound shame about her dependence, viewing it as weakness and spiritual failure that conflicted with Islamic principles of self-discipline and submission to Allah's will. She was terrified of her family and mosque community discovering her problem, fearing rejection and judgment.

She had tried to stop using medications through increased prayer and religious observance, but physical withdrawal symptoms and ongoing pain made abstinence impossible without professional support. This failure intensified her spiritual shame and self-criticism.

Rather than viewing her Islamic faith as obstacle to treatment, I worked to understand how her spiritual beliefs could support rather than hinder recovery efforts.

We explored Islamic concepts of balance, compassion, and Allah's mercy that could support self-forgiveness and realistic approaches to change. We discussed how seeking medical treatment for illness (including addiction) aligned with Islamic principles of caring for the body as a trust from Allah.

Amira found motivation for recovery in her desire to be a good Muslim wife and mother, to honor Allah through taking care of her health, and to serve her community more effectively.

We worked together to develop recovery strategies that aligned with Islamic practices. Her daily prayers became opportunities for spiritual grounding and intention-setting. Ramadan fasting (modified for her medical needs) became practice in self-discipline and spiritual connection.

When Amira felt ready, we involved her husband in treatment planning, educating him about addiction as illness rather than moral failure. We also connected with an imam who had experience with addiction counseling and could provide religious support for her recovery.

Six months later, Amira was successfully managing her pain through medical treatment while maintaining sobriety from addictive medications. Her faith had become a source of strength rather than shame, and she felt more connected to her spiritual community through honest relationships rather than fearful hiding.

Collaborating with Religious Leaders and Communities

Effective spiritual integration often requires building relationships with religious leaders and communities that can provide complementary support for therapeutic goals while maintaining appropriate professional boundaries.

Religious Leader Consultation can provide spiritual perspective, theological resources, and community support that enhance rather than compete with professional therapeutic services.

Many religious leaders have training in pastoral counseling, spiritual direction, or community care that complements professional therapy while providing religious resources that therapists cannot offer.

Some religious leaders might need education about mental health conditions, addiction, or therapeutic approaches to become effective collaborators rather than sources of conflict or misinformation.

Establishing relationships with religious leaders before crises develop creates resources that can be activated quickly when clients need integrated spiritual and professional support.

Faith Community Integration connects clients with religious communities that can provide ongoing support, accountability, and spiritual resources that complement professional treatment.

Religious communities often offer practical support like meals, childcare, or financial assistance that address social determinants of mental health while providing spiritual community and belonging.

Faith-based support groups, prayer groups, or spiritual direction programs might complement professional therapy while providing culturally and religiously appropriate peer support.

Some faith communities might need education about mental health stigma, addiction as illness, or appropriate ways to support community members receiving professional treatment.

Theological Resource Development involves learning enough about different religious traditions to identify spiritual resources that can support therapeutic goals while avoiding theological conflicts or inappropriate religious interpretation.

This doesn't mean becoming religious expert, but it does mean understanding basic theological concepts, spiritual practices, and religious resources that clients might find helpful for change processes.

Different religious traditions have different concepts of forgiveness, redemption, spiritual growth, and community support that can be integrated with therapeutic approaches when understood appropriately.

Using Spiritual Metaphors and Language in MI

Religious clients often respond better to therapeutic language that incorporates spiritual concepts and metaphors that resonate with their existing meaning-making systems and motivational frameworks.

Religious Language Integration involves using spiritual vocabulary that feels natural to religious clients while maintaining therapeutic accuracy and avoiding inappropriate religious interpretation or theological overstepping.

"How do you think God wants you to take care of yourself?" connects self-care to spiritual values rather than framing it as purely individual concern.

"What kind of witness do you want to be through how you handle this challenge?" connects change goals to spiritual identity and community representation rather than purely personal improvement.

"How might your faith community support you through this change process?" identifies religious resources while maintaining focus on therapeutic goals and change processes.

Scripture and Sacred Text Integration can provide motivational resources when clients find strength and guidance in religious teachings that support therapeutic goals.

Many religious traditions have teachings about healing, growth, forgiveness, and community support that can complement therapeutic approaches while providing spiritual grounding and motivation.

Working with religious texts requires understanding their appropriate interpretation and application rather than using them as therapeutic tools without religious knowledge or cultural competence.

Religious clients might find passages that support self-compassion, realistic goal-setting, or seeking help that can counter spiritual barriers or religious guilt that interfere with therapeutic progress.

Prayer and Meditation Integration allows clients to use familiar spiritual practices as therapeutic resources while maintaining appropriate professional boundaries around religious practice and spiritual direction.

Mindfulness and meditation practices have roots in many religious traditions and can be framed in spiritually familiar language while providing evidence-based mental health benefits.

Prayer practices might provide structure for reflection, intention-setting, and spiritual connection that support therapeutic goals while honoring religious identity and practice.

Working with prayer and meditation requires understanding the difference between therapeutic application and religious instruction while supporting client spiritual resources appropriately.

Addressing Conflicts Between Faith and Behavior Change Goals

Sometimes religious beliefs seem to conflict with therapeutic goals or evidence-based treatment approaches, requiring careful navigation that honors both spiritual values and effective treatment principles.

Theological Reframing helps clients find religious resources that support rather than hinder change efforts while maintaining theological integrity and spiritual authenticity.

Many religious traditions have teachings about compassion, healing, forgiveness, and growth that can support therapeutic approaches when understood appropriately within theological contexts.

Religious concepts of redemption, restoration, or spiritual transformation might provide motivational frameworks that support change efforts while maintaining spiritual identity and community connection.

Working with religious leaders or theological consultants can help identify spiritual resources that support therapeutic goals while addressing theological concerns or conflicts that might interfere with treatment.

Harm Reduction from Religious Perspectives might require finding spiritual frameworks that support gradual improvement and realistic goal-setting rather than perfectionist expectations that create failure cycles.

Many religious traditions emphasize progress over perfection, mercy over judgment, and practical wisdom over idealistic expectations that can support harm reduction approaches within spiritual contexts.

Religious concepts of stewardship, self-care, or community responsibility might support practical approaches to change that prioritize safety and health while working toward spiritual ideals.

Community Religious Education might be necessary when faith communities have stigmatizing attitudes or unrealistic expectations that interfere with members' ability to seek appropriate help or maintain realistic change goals.

This requires careful boundary management and appropriate consultation with religious leaders rather than directly challenging religious beliefs or community practices that exceed professional expertise.

Working with Different Religious Traditions

Effective spiritual integration requires understanding how different religious traditions approach mental health, change, and professional help in ways that influence therapeutic relationships and intervention strategies.

Christianity encompasses diverse denominations with different approaches to mental health, healing, and professional treatment that influence client attitudes and community resources.

Catholic traditions often emphasize sacramental healing, community support, and spiritual direction that can complement therapeutic approaches while providing religious resources for motivation and support.

Protestant traditions might emphasize personal relationship with Jesus, biblical guidance, and faith community support that can provide spiritual resources while potentially creating conflicts with professional treatment approaches.

Orthodox traditions often include rich spiritual practices, community liturgical life, and theological frameworks that can support healing when integrated appropriately with therapeutic work.

Islam provides comprehensive life guidance that can either support or complicate therapeutic approaches depending on how religious principles are understood and applied to mental health contexts.

Islamic principles of balance, community support, and submission to Allah's will can support therapeutic goals when understood within appropriate theological frameworks that honor both faith and health.

Muslim communities might have specific cultural considerations around gender, family involvement, and religious practice that influence therapeutic relationships and treatment approaches.

Judaism includes diverse traditions with different approaches to mental health, healing, and community support that can provide rich resources for therapeutic integration.

Jewish concepts of *tikkun olam* (repairing the world), community responsibility, and spiritual growth can support therapeutic goals while providing cultural and religious meaning frameworks.

Orthodox, Conservative, and Reform traditions might have different approaches to professional treatment and religious integration that require understanding and accommodation.

Buddhism and **Hinduism** include spiritual practices like meditation, mindfulness, and spiritual development that often complement therapeutic approaches while providing cultural and spiritual resources.

These traditions might have different concepts of suffering, attachment, and spiritual growth that can support therapeutic goals while providing alternative frameworks for understanding problems and change.

Indigenous Spiritual Traditions often include holistic approaches to healing that integrate mental, physical, spiritual, and community elements that can complement professional treatment when approached respectfully.

Training Implications for Spiritual Integration

Effective spiritual integration in MI requires specific knowledge and skills that should be included in professional development for therapists working in diverse religious communities.

Religious Literacy helps therapists understand basic concepts, practices, and resources from different religious traditions without becoming theological experts or religious practitioners.

Spiritual Assessment Skills include abilities to explore religious resources and barriers while maintaining appropriate professional boundaries and avoiding inappropriate religious interpretation or theological overstepping.

Religious Community Collaboration involves building relationships with religious leaders and communities that can provide complementary support for therapeutic goals while maintaining appropriate professional and religious boundaries.

Ethical Navigation addresses complex boundary issues that emerge when integrating spiritual and therapeutic approaches while maintaining professional competence and religious respectfulness.

What This Means for Your Practice

Spiritual integration in MI requires genuine respect for religious beliefs combined with clinical skills that can work within rather than against spiritual frameworks that provide meaning and motivation for many clients.

Spiritual Openness creates therapeutic environments where religious clients feel comfortable sharing spiritual resources and concerns without fear of judgment or religious dismissal.

Religious Collaboration involves working with rather than around spiritual beliefs while finding ways to integrate religious resources with evidence-based therapeutic approaches.

Boundary Clarity maintains appropriate professional limits while respecting spiritual authority and religious expertise that exceed therapeutic competence and training.

Cultural Competence includes understanding how different religious traditions approach mental health, change, and professional treatment in ways that influence therapeutic relationships and intervention effectiveness.

Most importantly, approach spiritual integration as collaborative work that honors both professional expertise and religious wisdom while supporting client goals that honor both health and spiritual authenticity.

When you can work skillfully within spiritual frameworks while maintaining MI's collaborative spirit, you create therapeutic relationships that feel spiritually congruent while providing professional resources that enhance rather than compete with religious faith and community support.

That's not just good therapy—it's respectful practice that honors the whole person within their spiritual context while supporting both psychological healing and spiritual growth.

Section IV: Systemic Applications

Chapter 14: Integrating Multiple Spiritual Practices

Different spiritual practices offer various resources for supporting change processes when integrated thoughtfully with MI approaches. Understanding how these practices function can help you support clients in accessing spiritual resources that align with their therapeutic goals.

Contemplative Practices like meditation, prayer, and spiritual reading provide structured approaches to reflection and intention-setting that can complement MI's focus on motivation and change planning.

These practices often include elements that support self-awareness, emotional regulation, and value clarification that directly enhance therapeutic work while providing spiritual grounding and connection.

Ritual and Ceremony might include religious services, spiritual retreats, or personal spiritual practices that provide meaning-making frameworks and community connection that support sustained change efforts.

Understanding how different spiritual traditions use ritual can help you support clients in accessing these resources appropriately while maintaining professional boundaries around religious practice and spiritual direction.

Community Worship and Fellowship provides social support, accountability, and spiritual encouragement that can significantly enhance therapeutic outcomes when integrated appropriately with professional treatment.

Religious communities often offer practical resources, emotional support, and spiritual guidance that complement therapeutic services while providing cultural and spiritual belonging that professional relationships cannot duplicate.

Addressing Spiritual Bypassing and Spiritual Materialism

Sometimes clients use spiritual beliefs or practices to avoid rather than support genuine change work, requiring therapeutic attention to how spirituality is being used in the change process.

Spiritual Bypassing occurs when clients use spiritual beliefs to avoid dealing with psychological or practical issues that require attention and action rather than spiritual explanation or transcendence.

"God will handle it" or "I just need more faith" might represent spiritual bypassing when they're used to avoid taking practical steps that could support change goals and therapeutic progress.

Working with spiritual bypassing requires honoring spiritual beliefs while exploring how spiritual and practical approaches can complement rather than replace each other in supporting comprehensive change efforts.

Spiritual Materialism involves using spiritual practices or beliefs as ego enhancement rather than genuine spiritual growth, which can interfere with the humility and openness required for therapeutic change.

This might manifest as spiritual superiority, religious perfectionism, or using spiritual identity to avoid examining problematic behaviors or attitudes that need attention in therapeutic work.

Balanced Spiritual Integration honors spiritual resources while maintaining focus on practical changes and psychological growth that support both spiritual and therapeutic goals without creating artificial conflicts between different aspects of healing.

Long-Term Spiritual Support for Sustained Change

Effective spiritual integration extends beyond individual therapeutic sessions to include ongoing spiritual resources and community support that can sustain change efforts over time.

Spiritual Community Development helps clients build or strengthen connections with religious communities that can provide ongoing support, accountability, and spiritual resources for maintaining change commitments.

This might involve helping clients find appropriate religious communities, connecting with spiritual mentors, or developing ongoing relationships with religious leaders who can provide continued guidance and support.

Personal Spiritual Practice Development supports clients in establishing or strengthening individual spiritual practices that can provide ongoing resources for motivation, reflection, and spiritual connection throughout their change journey.

These practices should be sustainable, personally meaningful, and integrated with rather than competing with other aspects of recovery and mental health maintenance.

Crisis Spiritual Resources help clients identify spiritual supports that can be activated during difficult periods when change motivation wavers or when spiritual doubts and struggles threaten progress.

Understanding how spiritual resources function during crisis periods helps clients prepare for challenges while building resilience through integrated spiritual and psychological supports.

Conclusion: The Sacred and the Therapeutic

Spiritual integration in MI represents a fundamental recognition that for many clients, faith isn't optional—it's the foundation from which all other aspects of life, including change efforts, derive meaning and motivation.

This doesn't mean therapists need to become religious experts or spiritual directors. It means recognizing the legitimate role that spiritual resources can play in healing and change while maintaining appropriate professional boundaries and therapeutic focus.

The most effective spiritual integration happens when therapists approach religious beliefs with genuine curiosity and respect while finding ways to connect spiritual resources with evidence-based therapeutic approaches that support both psychological healing and spiritual growth.

This work requires ongoing education, consultation with religious leaders and communities, and careful attention to ethical boundaries that honor both professional competence and spiritual authority.

But for clients whose faith provides meaning, community, and motivation for change, this integration can transform therapeutic work from competing with spiritual resources to enhancing them, creating comprehensive approaches to healing that honor both psychological and spiritual dimensions of human experience.

That's the promise of spiritual integration in MI—not choosing between therapeutic and spiritual approaches, but finding ways to weave them together in service of comprehensive healing that honors the whole person within their spiritual context.

The integration of spirituality into MI practice represents both an opportunity and a challenge for mental health professionals working in diverse communities. When approached with cultural humility, professional competence, and genuine respect for religious wisdom, this integration can create therapeutic relationships that feel spiritually congruent while providing evidence-based resources for lasting change.

The key is approaching spiritual integration as collaborative work that honors both professional expertise and religious authority while maintaining focus on client goals that support both psychological health and spiritual authenticity. When therapists can work skillfully within these frameworks, they create opportunities for healing that addresses both individual symptoms and spiritual dimensions of human flourishing.

This comprehensive approach to spiritual integration doesn't replace professional therapeutic competence—it enhances it by acknowledging and working with the spiritual resources that many clients bring to the change process. That's culturally responsive therapy at its best, honoring both professional knowledge and spiritual wisdom in service of comprehensive healing and authentic change.

Chapter 15: Creating Inclusive MI Programs

When the mental health center where I consulted decided to become "culturally competent," they started with good intentions and a $50,000 budget for diversity training. Six months later, they had colorful posters on the walls, a few translated brochures, and staff who had attended workshops on cultural awareness. But their client demographics hadn't changed, their dropout rates for clients of color remained high, and their staff still felt unprepared to work with diverse populations.

"We don't understand," the clinical director told me. "We did the training. We hired a diversity consultant. We even got some artwork that represents different cultures. Why aren't we seeing results?"

The problem wasn't lack of effort—it was fundamental misunderstanding of what cultural responsiveness actually requires. They had focused on surface-level changes while leaving the deeper organizational structures, policies, and practices unchanged. They had approached cultural competence as a training problem rather than an organizational transformation challenge.

Creating truly inclusive MI programs requires much more than cultural awareness training or demographic representation. It requires systematic organizational change that affects everything from hiring practices to clinical protocols, from physical environments to community partnerships, from supervision approaches to outcome measurement.

This kind of organizational cultural humility doesn't happen overnight, and it can't be achieved through one-time initiatives or add-on programs. It requires sustained commitment to examining and changing organizational culture, structures, and practices that can either support or undermine culturally responsive MI practice.

Conducting Organizational Cultural Assessments

Before you can create cultural change, you need to understand your organization's current cultural responsiveness across all levels of operation, from individual staff competence to systemic policies and community relationships.

Staff Cultural Competence Assessment goes beyond demographic data to examine actual skills, knowledge, and attitudes that affect clinical work with diverse populations.

This includes assessing language capabilities, cultural knowledge about specific populations served, experience working across cultural differences, and comfort levels with cultural adaptation of MI techniques.

But it also includes examining implicit biases, cultural assumptions, and areas where staff need additional training or support to work effectively with diverse clients.

Staff assessment should be ongoing rather than one-time evaluation, recognizing that cultural competence develops over time and requires continuous learning and skill development.

Organizational Policy Review examines how written and unwritten policies either support or create barriers to cultural responsiveness in MI practice.

Do intake forms include culturally appropriate questions? Are scheduling policies flexible enough to accommodate different cultural time orientations or family involvement expectations? Do confidentiality policies account for cultural differences in family decision-making and information sharing?

Are treatment planning processes individualistic in ways that might conflict with collectivist cultural values? Do documentation requirements accommodate cultural adaptations of MI techniques?

Policy review should include both formal written policies and informal practices that affect how services are delivered and experienced by clients from different cultural backgrounds.

Physical Environment Assessment evaluates whether organizational spaces communicate cultural welcome and inclusivity or inadvertently create barriers for clients from different backgrounds.

This includes artwork, reading materials, signage, and physical arrangements that either reflect cultural diversity or suggest that certain cultural groups are more welcome than others.

But it also includes practical considerations like prayer spaces, family gathering areas, accessibility features, and environmental factors that affect comfort and engagement for different cultural groups.

Service Delivery Analysis examines how services are actually provided to different cultural groups, looking at utilization patterns, engagement rates, completion rates, and outcome differences across cultural populations.

Are certain cultural groups underrepresented in services? Do clients from different backgrounds have different patterns of service utilization or different outcomes? What might explain these differences?

This analysis should include both quantitative data about service patterns and qualitative information about client experiences and staff perspectives on cultural responsiveness.

Creating Systematic Organizational Change

Effective organizational cultural humility requires systematic change processes that address multiple levels of organizational functioning simultaneously rather than focusing on isolated interventions.

Leadership Commitment and Accountability forms the foundation for sustainable cultural change, requiring explicit commitment from organizational leaders combined with accountability systems that ensure progress over time.

Leadership commitment means more than verbal support for diversity initiatives. It means dedicating resources, changing policies, and making difficult decisions that prioritize cultural responsiveness even when it requires additional time, money, or effort.

It also means creating accountability systems that track progress on cultural responsiveness goals and hold leaders responsible for achieving measurable improvements in cultural inclusivity and effectiveness.

Cultural Change Implementation Teams should include representatives from all levels of the organization, community members, and cultural consultants who can guide comprehensive change processes.

These teams need authority to examine and recommend changes to policies, procedures, training programs, and service delivery approaches that affect cultural responsiveness.

They also need resources, timelines, and support systems that enable them to conduct thorough organizational assessment and implement sustainable changes rather than surface-level modifications.

Phased Implementation Strategies recognize that organizational cultural change takes time and requires careful sequencing of different change initiatives to build momentum and competence over time.

Early phases might focus on immediate barriers to cultural access while later phases address more complex issues like cultural adaptation of clinical protocols or community partnership development.

Each phase should build on previous changes while preparing the foundation for more advanced cultural responsiveness initiatives.

Case Study: Transforming an Organizational Culture

Let me share a detailed example of how comprehensive organizational cultural transformation worked at a community mental health center that served a rapidly diversifying urban area.

Valley Community Mental Health had been serving a predominantly white, English-speaking population for thirty years. But demographic changes in their catchment area meant they were now supposed to serve Latino, African American, Somali, and Vietnamese communities that had little connection to their services.

Initial attempts at cultural responsiveness included hiring bilingual staff, translating brochures, and providing basic cultural awareness training. But utilization by communities of color remained low, and clients who did access services often dropped out after a few sessions.

The executive director realized they needed systematic organizational transformation rather than add-on cultural initiatives. She committed to a three-year cultural responsiveness initiative with dedicated funding and leadership accountability.

The first step was comprehensive organizational assessment that included staff competence evaluation, policy review, environmental assessment, and extensive community input about barriers to service access and cultural responsiveness.

The assessment revealed multiple systemic barriers: intake processes designed for individual decision-making that felt foreign to collectivist cultures, scheduling policies that didn't accommodate family involvement or cultural time orientations, physical environments that felt institutional and unwelcoming, and staff who felt unprepared to adapt clinical approaches for cultural differences.

The transformation plan addressed these barriers systematically. They redesigned intake processes to accommodate family involvement and cultural assessment. They implemented flexible scheduling that honored cultural time patterns and family consultation needs.

They created culturally welcoming physical environments with artwork, reading materials, and gathering spaces that reflected the communities they served. They developed comprehensive cultural competence training that went beyond awareness to include practical skills for cultural adaptation of MI and other therapeutic approaches.

Most importantly, they established community partnerships with cultural organizations, religious institutions, and informal community leaders who could provide cultural consultation and help bridge between professional services and community resources.

Three years later, their client demographics reflected their community diversity, dropout rates had decreased significantly across all cultural groups, and staff reported feeling confident and skilled in culturally responsive MI practice.

The transformation required substantial investment and organizational commitment, but it resulted in both improved community health outcomes and increased staff satisfaction and competence.

Training Programs for Culturally Responsive MI

Effective cultural competence training goes beyond general cultural awareness to include specific skills for adapting MI techniques and approaches for different cultural contexts.

Foundational Cultural Knowledge provides essential background about different cultural groups served by the organization while avoiding stereotypes or overgeneralizations that could interfere with individualized cultural assessment.

This includes basic information about cultural values, communication patterns, family structures, religious influences, and historical experiences that might influence therapeutic relationships and MI effectiveness.

But it also emphasizes cultural diversity within groups and individual variation that requires assessment and cultural curiosity rather than assumption-making based on ethnic or cultural background.

MI Cultural Adaptation Skills teach specific techniques for modifying standard MI approaches to work effectively within different cultural contexts while maintaining therapeutic effectiveness.

This includes training in cultural assessment, adapting communication styles, working with interpreters, including family members appropriately, and integrating spiritual and cultural resources into change planning.

It also includes practice opportunities for applying these skills with different cultural scenarios and receiving feedback on cultural responsiveness and clinical effectiveness.

Cultural Self-Awareness Development helps staff examine their own cultural identities, biases, and assumptions that influence their clinical work and cultural interactions.

This isn't about creating guilt or defensiveness but about developing the self-awareness necessary for effective cross-cultural work and cultural adaptation of therapeutic approaches.

Community Cultural Consultation connects staff with community cultural resources and consultation opportunities that can enhance their cultural knowledge and provide ongoing support for culturally responsive practice.

This might include relationships with cultural organizations, religious leaders, community elders, or cultural consultants who can provide guidance about specific cultural adaptations or community resources.

Policy and Procedure Development

Creating culturally responsive MI programs requires developing policies and procedures that institutionalize cultural responsiveness rather than leaving it dependent on individual staff initiative or cultural awareness.

Culturally Responsive Intake Processes ensure that initial client contact includes appropriate cultural assessment while accommodating different cultural approaches to help-seeking and information sharing.

Intake forms should include questions about cultural background, language preferences, family involvement preferences, and cultural resources that might support therapeutic goals.

But intake processes should also be flexible enough to accommodate cultural differences in information sharing, decision-making, and help-seeking patterns that might not fit standard intake procedures.

Cultural Accommodation Policies provide clear guidelines for accommodating cultural needs like interpreters, family involvement, religious considerations, and cultural modifications of treatment approaches.

These policies should specify how to access interpretation services, when family involvement is appropriate and how to manage it, how to accommodate religious practices and considerations, and how to modify treatment approaches for cultural appropriateness.

They should also address resource allocation, staff training needs, and quality assurance for culturally adapted services.

Staff Cultural Competence Requirements establish expectations and accountability systems for cultural knowledge, skills, and attitudes that support effective cross-cultural MI practice.

This might include cultural competence standards for hiring, ongoing training requirements, supervision expectations, and performance evaluation criteria that include cultural responsiveness indicators.

Community Partnership Protocols provide frameworks for developing and maintaining relationships with cultural communities and organizations that can support culturally responsive services.

These protocols should address how to identify appropriate community partners, how to develop collaborative relationships, how to maintain cultural partnerships over time, and how to evaluate partnership effectiveness.

Community Partnership Development

Sustainable culturally responsive MI programs require ongoing partnerships with cultural communities rather than attempting to provide services in isolation from community cultural resources and leadership.

Community Cultural Assessment involves systematic outreach to understand community cultural resources, leadership structures, help-seeking patterns, and barriers to professional mental health service utilization.

This assessment should be conducted in partnership with community members rather than as research done on communities, ensuring that community perspectives and priorities guide partnership development.

Cultural Leader Engagement builds relationships with formal and informal community leaders who can provide cultural consultation, community education, and bridge-building between professional services and community resources.

These relationships require long-term commitment, mutual respect, and shared decision-making rather than one-way consultation that extracts cultural knowledge without providing community benefit.

Collaborative Service Development creates opportunities for communities to influence service design, delivery approaches, and outcome evaluation rather than simply receiving services designed by professional providers.

This might include community advisory boards, cultural consultation in treatment planning, community-based service delivery, or collaborative program evaluation that includes community-defined success indicators.

Cultural Resource Integration connects professional MI services with existing community cultural resources rather than competing with or replacing community support systems.

This requires understanding and working with traditional healing practices, religious resources, cultural mentorship programs, and community support systems that can complement rather than conflict with professional therapeutic services.

Staff Development and Support Systems

Creating culturally responsive MI programs requires ongoing staff development and support systems that enable sustained cultural competence rather than one-time training initiatives.

Ongoing Cultural Education provides continuous learning opportunities about cultural competence, community changes, and emerging cultural issues that affect service delivery effectiveness.

This education should be responsive to community demographic changes, staff cultural learning needs, and emerging research about cultural adaptation of MI and other therapeutic approaches.

Cultural Consultation and Supervision ensures that staff have ongoing support for navigating cultural challenges, adapting MI techniques appropriately, and working effectively with diverse populations.

This might include cultural consultants, culturally competent supervisors, or peer consultation groups focused on cultural responsiveness and cross-cultural clinical effectiveness.

Staff Support for Cultural Stress recognizes that cross-cultural work can be challenging and provides support systems that help staff manage cultural conflicts, bias challenges, and the emotional demands of working across significant cultural differences.

Career Development Opportunities in cultural competence provide advancement opportunities for staff who develop expertise in culturally responsive MI practice while retaining experienced culturally competent staff within the organization.

Quality Assurance and Continuous Improvement

Culturally responsive MI programs require ongoing quality assurance and improvement processes that ensure cultural responsiveness is maintained and improved over time rather than declining due to staff turnover or organizational changes.

Cultural Responsiveness Monitoring tracks indicators of cultural effectiveness including demographic representation, engagement rates, completion rates, and outcome differences across cultural groups served.

This monitoring should be ongoing rather than annual and should trigger investigation and intervention when cultural disparities or barriers are identified.

Client Cultural Satisfaction Assessment provides systematic feedback from clients about cultural responsiveness, cultural accommodation, and cultural effectiveness of services received.

This assessment should be culturally appropriate, available in relevant languages, and designed to capture cultural experiences that might not be reflected in standard satisfaction measures.

Community Feedback Systems create ongoing opportunities for community input about service quality, cultural responsiveness, and community needs that might require service modifications or expansion.

Organizational Cultural Climate Assessment evaluates staff experiences of organizational support for cultural responsiveness, cultural competence development, and cross-cultural effectiveness.

This assessment can identify organizational barriers to cultural responsiveness that need attention as well as organizational strengths that support culturally responsive practice.

Technology and Cultural Responsiveness

Technology platforms and tools used for MI service delivery need careful consideration for cultural responsiveness to ensure they enhance rather than create barriers to culturally effective services.

Culturally Responsive Technology Selection considers how different technologies might be received by different cultural groups and whether they support or interfere with cultural values and communication patterns.

Some cultures might prefer phone contact over video platforms. Others might have technology access or comfort issues that require alternative service delivery approaches.

Language and Cultural Content in Technology ensures that technology platforms accommodate multiple languages and cultural communication patterns rather than assuming English-only or Western communication preferences.

Cultural Privacy and Security Considerations address how technology use intersects with cultural values about privacy, family involvement, and information sharing that might differ across cultural groups.

Measuring Organizational Cultural Competence

Effective organizational cultural humility requires systematic measurement of cultural responsiveness at organizational levels rather than focusing only on individual staff cultural competence.

Organizational Cultural Competence Indicators might include demographic representation in services, cultural satisfaction ratings, staff cultural competence assessments, community partnership quality, and cultural adaptation of service protocols.

Benchmark Comparison with other organizations serving similar populations can provide external standards for organizational cultural responsiveness and identify areas for improvement or best practices to adopt.

Longitudinal Cultural Progress Tracking monitors organizational cultural development over time to ensure sustainable progress rather than short-term improvements that don't persist.

What This Means for Your Organization

Creating organizationally culturally responsive MI programs requires systematic commitment to change that affects all levels of organizational functioning rather than focusing on individual cultural competence or add-on diversity initiatives.

Leadership Commitment must be genuine and sustained, with dedicated resources, accountability systems, and willingness to make difficult changes that prioritize cultural responsiveness even when it requires additional investment.

Systematic Change Approach addresses multiple organizational levels simultaneously rather than focusing on isolated interventions that don't create comprehensive cultural transformation.

Community Partnership ensures that cultural responsiveness is guided by and accountable to the communities served rather than developed in isolation from community input and cultural expertise.

Long-term Perspective recognizes that organizational cultural change takes time and requires sustained effort rather than expecting immediate results from short-term initiatives.

Quality Assurance Systems ensure that cultural responsiveness is maintained and improved over time rather than declining due to staff turnover, funding pressures, or competing organizational priorities.

Most importantly, approach organizational cultural humility as ongoing commitment to serving all community members effectively rather than one-time project or compliance requirement.

When organizations can create systematically culturally responsive environments for MI practice, they provide opportunities for effective services that feel culturally authentic to clients while supporting professional effectiveness for staff. That's not just good cultural competence—it's organizational excellence that serves both individual clients and community health effectively.

Organizational cultural humility represents a fundamental shift from viewing cultural competence as individual staff responsibility to understanding it as organizational commitment that requires systematic change and ongoing accountability.

This shift requires leadership courage, resource commitment, and willingness to examine and change organizational practices that might inadvertently create cultural barriers or disparities in service effectiveness.

But organizations that make this commitment often find that cultural responsiveness enhances rather than complicates service delivery, creating more effective therapeutic relationships while expanding community access and engagement.

The result is organizations that can serve increasingly diverse communities effectively while providing professionally satisfying work environments that attract and retain culturally competent staff committed to community service and cultural responsiveness.

Chapter 16: Measuring Cultural Responsiveness

Assessment Tools and Outcomes

When the community health center I worked with received a large federal grant to improve services for Latino families, they were required to demonstrate "culturally appropriate outcomes" to maintain their funding. The problem? They had no idea how to measure cultural responsiveness, and standard outcome measures didn't capture whether their services felt culturally authentic or effective to the families they served.

"We can show you that depression scores improved," the program director told the grant reviewers. "We can document session attendance and treatment completion rates. But how do we prove that families felt understood and respected as Latino families rather than just as depression cases?"

The reviewers pushed back. "Standard measures should be sufficient. Depression is depression, right? Cultural factors are interesting, but the real outcomes are symptom reduction and functional improvement."

But the community health center was right to be concerned. Six months later, despite showing good outcomes on standard measures, their Latino client retention rates were terrible. Families would attend a few sessions, show some improvement, and then disappear. Exit interviews revealed that while families appreciated symptom relief, they didn't feel that treatment honored their cultural values or connected with their actual lived experiences as Latino families.

This experience highlights a crucial challenge in culturally responsive MI: How do you measure cultural effectiveness in ways that capture both clinical outcomes and cultural authenticity? How do you demonstrate that services are not just clinically effective but culturally responsive?

Existing Measures of Cultural Competence in MI

Traditional outcome measures in mental health focus on symptom reduction, functional improvement, and treatment retention without addressing cultural responsiveness or cultural fit of therapeutic approaches.

Clinical Outcome Limitations become apparent when standard measures show good results but clients don't feel culturally understood or when treatment gains don't generalize to clients' cultural contexts and community relationships.

Depression inventories, anxiety scales, and functional assessments might miss cultural factors that influence symptoms, recovery processes, and sustainable change within clients' actual cultural environments.

Standard MI measures like motivation rulers or change commitment scales might not capture cultural factors that influence motivation, such as family considerations, cultural values, or community expectations that affect individual change processes.

Cultural Competence Assessment Tools have been developed for general mental health practice but need adaptation for MI-specific approaches and cultural considerations.

The Cultural Competence Self-Assessment Tool (CCSAT) and similar instruments focus on provider cultural knowledge and attitudes but don't specifically address MI cultural adaptation skills or cultural responsiveness in motivational interviewing techniques.

The Intercultural Development Inventory (IDI) measures intercultural competence but doesn't address specific clinical skills for cultural adaptation of therapeutic approaches or MI-specific cultural responsiveness.

MI-Specific Cultural Measures are limited and often don't capture the cultural aspects of motivational interviewing that determine whether MI approaches feel culturally authentic and effective to clients from different backgrounds.

Existing MI fidelity measures like the Motivational Interviewing Treatment Integrity (MITI) code don't include cultural responsiveness indicators or cultural adaptation competencies that determine MI effectiveness across cultural contexts.

Developing Culturally Appropriate Outcome Measures

Creating meaningful measures of cultural responsiveness in MI requires developing assessment approaches that capture both clinical effectiveness and cultural authenticity within clients' actual cultural contexts.

Cultural Fit Assessment measures whether MI approaches align with clients' cultural values, communication patterns, decision-making processes, and meaning-making systems.

This might include questions about whether therapeutic approaches felt culturally familiar, whether cultural values were honored in treatment planning, and whether changes felt authentic within clients' cultural contexts.

"Did your counselor understand how your family background influenced your situation?" or "Did the changes you made honor your cultural values?" capture cultural authenticity that standard outcome measures miss.

Cultural Resource Integration measures how well therapeutic approaches connected with and enhanced clients' existing cultural resources rather than competing with or replacing them.

This includes assessment of whether MI approaches integrated with religious resources, family support systems, cultural wisdom, or community connections that provide meaning and support for clients' change processes.

"Did counseling help you use your faith/family/community resources better?" captures cultural resource enhancement that contributes to sustainable change within cultural contexts.

Cultural Empowerment Outcomes assess whether MI approaches enhanced clients' cultural identity, community connections, and ability to navigate between different cultural contexts effectively.

Some clients need to develop bicultural competence, strengthen cultural identity, or improve their ability to advocate for cultural needs within mainstream systems. These outcomes might be as important as symptom reduction for long-term well-being.

Family and Community Impact Measures capture whether individual changes strengthened rather than strained cultural relationships and community connections that provide ongoing support and meaning.

Traditional individual outcome measures might miss whether changes enhanced family harmony, improved community standing, or strengthened cultural connections that determine long-term sustainability of therapeutic gains.

Case Study: Comprehensive Cultural Outcome Assessment

Let me share a detailed example of how comprehensive cultural outcome assessment worked with a program serving Vietnamese refugee families dealing with trauma and acculturation stress.

Traditional PTSD measures showed good symptom reduction, but program staff noticed that clients often stopped attending sessions once symptoms improved, even when they still struggled with cultural conflicts and family stresses that seemed related to their original trauma.

The program developed a comprehensive cultural outcome assessment that included standard clinical measures plus cultural responsiveness indicators, cultural resource integration measures, and community impact assessments.

The cultural measures revealed that while PTSD symptoms improved, clients often felt that treatment hadn't addressed their cultural shame about needing help, their conflicts between traditional Vietnamese values and American expectations, or their struggles with maintaining cultural identity while adapting to new cultural contexts.

Clients reported that while they felt better individually, they weren't sure how to maintain improvements within their families and cultural communities where different values and expectations might not support the changes they had made in therapy.

The program used this information to modify their approach, including more family involvement, more explicit cultural assessment and adaptation, and more attention to how individual changes could be sustained within Vietnamese cultural contexts and family relationships.

Six-month follow-up assessments showed that both clinical outcomes and cultural outcomes improved when treatment addressed cultural as well as individual factors, and that clients maintained gains better when changes were integrated with rather than separate from their cultural identities and community connections.

Client Feedback Systems for Cultural Responsiveness

Systematic client feedback about cultural responsiveness provides essential information about whether MI approaches feel culturally appropriate and effective from clients' perspectives rather than just professional assumptions about cultural effectiveness.

Cultural Satisfaction Assessment goes beyond general satisfaction to assess specific cultural aspects of therapeutic relationships and intervention approaches.

"Did your counselor understand your cultural background?" "Did you feel comfortable being yourself culturally during sessions?" "Did the counseling approach fit with your cultural values?" capture cultural satisfaction that general measures might miss.

Cultural Accommodation Feedback assesses how well services accommodated cultural needs like language preferences, family involvement, religious considerations, or cultural time orientations.

"Were you able to include family members when you wanted to?" "Did scheduling accommodate your cultural or religious obligations?" "Were cultural dietary or religious restrictions respected?" provide feedback about cultural accommodation effectiveness.

Cultural Change Process Assessment evaluates whether change processes felt culturally authentic and whether changes were integrated successfully within clients' cultural contexts and relationships.

"Did the changes you made fit with your cultural values?" "How did your family/community respond to the changes you made?" "Do the changes feel sustainable within your cultural context?" assess cultural authenticity of change processes.

Cultural Empowerment Feedback captures whether therapeutic processes enhanced cultural identity, community connections, and cultural competence rather than requiring cultural assimilation or identity suppression.

"Did counseling help you feel more confident about your cultural identity?" "Are you better able to navigate between different cultural contexts?" assess cultural empowerment outcomes that contribute to long-term well-being.

Measuring Cultural Adaptation Fidelity

Just as standard MI requires fidelity measures to ensure intervention quality, culturally adapted MI needs measures that assess whether cultural adaptations are implemented appropriately and effectively.

Cultural Assessment Fidelity measures whether practitioners conduct adequate cultural assessment and use cultural information appropriately in treatment planning and intervention modification.

This includes assessment of cultural assessment depth, accuracy of cultural understanding, and appropriate integration of cultural information into MI approaches and treatment planning.

Cultural Technique Adaptation measures how well practitioners modify MI techniques for cultural appropriateness while maintaining therapeutic effectiveness and MI spirit.

This might include assessment of communication style adaptation, family involvement integration, spiritual resource inclusion, and cultural metaphor or language use that enhances rather than compromises MI effectiveness.

Cultural Relationship Building assesses practitioners' ability to build therapeutic relationships that feel culturally authentic and respectful to clients from different cultural backgrounds.

This includes measures of cultural humility, cultural curiosity, cultural respect, and ability to navigate cultural differences effectively while maintaining therapeutic alliance and collaborative MI relationships.

Cultural Resource Integration measures how well practitioners identify and integrate clients' cultural resources rather than working around or against cultural factors that could support therapeutic goals.

Research Considerations for Diverse Populations

Conducting research on culturally responsive MI requires methodological considerations that ensure research approaches are culturally appropriate and that findings are applicable to diverse cultural contexts.

Culturally Responsive Research Design must consider how research participation, data collection methods, and outcome measurement might be perceived and experienced differently across cultural groups.

Some cultures might view research participation as inappropriate sharing of family information. Others might have different comfort levels with questionnaires, interviews, or behavioral observations that affect data quality and cultural appropriateness.

Research designs should include cultural community input in planning, culturally appropriate consent processes, and data collection methods that feel respectful and meaningful to participants from different cultural backgrounds.

Cultural Measurement Equivalence ensures that measures assess the same constructs across different cultural groups rather than reflecting cultural differences in expression or understanding that could be misinterpreted as clinical differences.

Depression might be expressed differently across cultures, with some emphasizing somatic symptoms and others emphasizing emotional symptoms. Anxiety might be understood as spiritual problems in some cultures and medical problems in others.

Establishing cultural measurement equivalence requires careful translation processes, cultural adaptation of items, and validation with different cultural groups to ensure measures assess intended constructs rather than cultural differences in symptom expression.

Cultural Sampling and Recruitment must ensure adequate representation of cultural groups while avoiding cultural stereotyping or assumption-making about cultural homogeneity within ethnic or racial categories.

Latino populations include multiple national origins, immigration experiences, socioeconomic levels, and cultural orientations that might influence research participation and outcome patterns. Asian populations include dozens of distinct cultural groups with different languages, religious traditions, and cultural values.

Research sampling should acknowledge cultural diversity within broad ethnic categories while ensuring adequate representation for meaningful cultural analysis.

Cultural Data Interpretation requires understanding how cultural factors might influence research findings in ways that could be misinterpreted if cultural context isn't considered appropriately.

Lower treatment utilization by certain cultural groups might reflect cultural barriers rather than lack of need. Different outcome patterns might reflect cultural differences in change processes rather than intervention effectiveness differences.

Cultural interpretation requires collaboration with cultural community members and cultural experts who can help understand findings within appropriate cultural contexts.

Technology-Based Cultural Assessment

Digital platforms and mobile applications create new opportunities for cultural responsiveness assessment while also raising questions about cultural appropriateness of technology-based measurement approaches.

Cultural Technology Comfort varies across different populations, with some cultural groups more comfortable with digital assessment while others prefer in-person or paper-based approaches.

Age, education, immigration status, and cultural background all influence technology comfort and access that affect the cultural appropriateness and feasibility of technology-based cultural assessment approaches.

Language and Cultural Content in digital assessments must accommodate multiple languages and cultural concepts that might not translate directly or might require cultural explanation for appropriate understanding and response.

Cultural Privacy Considerations become more complex with digital assessment when cultural groups have different expectations about information privacy, family involvement in health decisions, or appropriate sharing of personal information through technology platforms.

Building Cultural Outcome Measurement Systems

Creating comprehensive systems for measuring cultural responsiveness requires integrating multiple assessment approaches that capture different aspects of cultural effectiveness over time.

Multi-Perspective Assessment includes client perspectives, family perspectives, community perspectives, and practitioner perspectives on cultural responsiveness and cultural effectiveness of MI approaches.

These different perspectives might reveal different aspects of cultural effectiveness that single-perspective assessment would miss while providing more comprehensive understanding of cultural responsiveness.

Longitudinal Cultural Tracking follows cultural outcomes over time to assess whether cultural gains are maintained and whether cultural integration of changes supports long-term well-being within clients' actual cultural contexts.

Short-term cultural satisfaction might not predict long-term cultural sustainability of changes, requiring follow-up assessment that captures cultural effectiveness over time rather than just immediate post-treatment cultural satisfaction.

Cultural Quality Improvement Integration uses cultural outcome data to continuously improve cultural responsiveness of MI programs rather than just documenting cultural effectiveness for reporting purposes.

This requires systems that can identify cultural barriers, track cultural improvement efforts, and modify programs based on cultural effectiveness data rather than just clinical outcome data.

Training Implications for Cultural Measurement

Effective cultural outcome measurement requires training for practitioners, supervisors, and program administrators who need to understand both clinical and cultural indicators of MI effectiveness.

Cultural Assessment Training helps practitioners understand how to gather and interpret cultural outcome information while maintaining appropriate cultural humility and avoiding cultural stereotyping or over-interpretation of cultural data.

Cultural Data Interpretation training helps supervisors and administrators understand how to use cultural outcome data for program improvement while avoiding cultural deficit interpretations that blame cultural factors rather than examining cultural responsiveness of services.

Cultural Quality Improvement training integrates cultural outcome data with program development processes that can enhance cultural responsiveness based on systematic cultural effectiveness assessment.

What This Means for Your Practice

Measuring cultural responsiveness in MI requires expanding outcome assessment beyond standard clinical measures to include cultural authenticity, cultural resource integration, and cultural sustainability of change processes.

Cultural Outcome Integration makes cultural effectiveness as important as clinical effectiveness in determining MI program success and quality improvement priorities.

Client Cultural Perspective prioritizes client cultural experience and cultural satisfaction as legitimate and important indicators of MI effectiveness that deserve systematic attention and program response.

Cultural Sustainability Focus emphasizes long-term cultural integration of changes rather than just short-term clinical improvement that might not be maintained within clients' actual cultural contexts and relationships.

Continuous Cultural Improvement uses cultural outcome data for ongoing program enhancement that improves cultural responsiveness over time rather than accepting cultural barriers as unchangeable program limitations.

Most importantly, approach cultural outcome measurement as quality improvement tool that enhances both cultural responsiveness and clinical effectiveness rather than additional compliance requirement that competes with clinical goals.

When measurement systems can capture both clinical effectiveness and cultural authenticity, they provide information that helps MI programs serve diverse communities more effectively while maintaining therapeutic integrity and cultural respect.

That's not just good measurement—it's culturally responsive evaluation that supports both individual healing and community health through services that honor both professional competence and cultural wisdom.

Advancing the Field

Cultural responsiveness measurement represents an emerging area of MI research and practice that requires ongoing development, validation, and refinement to serve increasingly diverse communities effectively.

This work requires collaboration between researchers, practitioners, and cultural communities to develop measures that capture cultural effectiveness in ways that feel meaningful and respectful to the communities served.

The goal isn't just better measurement but better services that can demonstrate both clinical effectiveness and cultural authenticity in ways that build community trust and support sustainable therapeutic relationships across cultural differences.

That's the promise of comprehensive cultural outcome measurement—services that work both clinically and culturally, creating healing opportunities that honor both professional expertise and cultural wisdom in service of comprehensive well-being for increasingly diverse communities.

References

1. Miller, W. R., & Rollnick, S. (2013). *Motivational interviewing: Helping people change* (3rd ed.). Guilford Press.

2. Sue, D. W., & Sue, D. (2015). *Counseling the culturally diverse: Theory and practice* (7th ed.). Wiley.

3. Hettema, J., Steele, J., & Miller, W. R. (2005). Motivational interviewing. *Annual Review of Clinical Psychology*, 1, 91-111.

4. Castro, F. G., Barrera, M., & Holleran Steiker, L. K. (2010). Issues and challenges in the design of culturally adapted evidence-based interventions. *Annual Review of Clinical Psychology*, 6, 213-239.

5. Triandis, H. C. (1995). *Individualism and collectivism*. Westview Press.

6. Resnicow, K., Baranowski, T., Ahluwalia, J. S., & Braithwaite, R. L. (1999). Cultural sensitivity in public health: Defined and demystified. *Ethnicity & Disease*, 9(1), 10-21.

7. Bernal, G., & Sáez-Santiago, E. (2006). Culturally centered psychosocial interventions. *Journal of Community Psychology*, 34(2), 121-132.

8. Hall, G. C. N., Ibaraki, A. Y., Huang, E. R., Marti, C. N., & Stice, E. (2016). A meta-analysis of cultural adaptations of prevention programs for Asian American youth. *Clinical Psychology Review*, 45, 72-83.

9. Cabassa, L. J., & Baumann, A. A. (2013). A two-way street: Bridging implementation science and cultural adaptations of mental health treatments. *Implementation Science*, 8, 90.

10. Falicov, C. J. (2009). Commentary: On the wisdom and challenges of culturally attuned treatments for Latinos. *Family Process*, 48(2), 292-309.

11. Tervalon, M., & Murray-García, J. (1998). Cultural humility versus cultural competence: A critical distinction in defining physician training outcomes in multicultural education. *Journal of Health Care for the Poor and Underserved*, 9(2), 117-125.

12. Falicov, C. J. (2014). *Latino families in therapy* (2nd ed.). Guilford Press.

13. McGoldrick, M., Giordano, J., & Garcia-Preto, N. (2005). *Ethnicity and family therapy* (3rd ed.). Guilford Press.

14. Hofstede, G. (2001). *Culture's consequences: Comparing values, behaviors, institutions and organizations across nations* (2nd ed.). Sage.

15. Berry, J. W. (2005). Acculturation: Living successfully in two cultures. *International Journal of Intercultural Relations*, 29(6), 697-712.

16. Bronfenbrenner, U. (1979). *The ecology of human development: Experiments by nature and design*. Harvard University Press.

17. Kleinman, A., Eisenberg, L., & Good, B. (1978). Culture, illness, and care: Clinical lessons from anthropologic and cross-cultural research. *Annals of Internal Medicine*, 88(2), 251-258.

18. Paniagua, F. A. (2014). *Assessing and treating culturally diverse clients: A practical guide* (4th ed.). Sage.

19. Cardemil, E. V. (2010). Cultural adaptations to empirically supported treatments: A research agenda. *The Scientific Review of Mental Health Practice*, 7(2), 8-21.

20. Greenwald, A. G., & Banaji, M. R. (1995). Implicit social cognition: Attitudes, self-esteem, and stereotypes. *Psychological Review*, 102(1), 4-27.

21. Williams, D. R., & Mohammed, S. A. (2009). Discrimination and racial disparities in health: Evidence and needed research. *Journal of Behavioral Medicine*, 32(1), 20-47.

22. Koenig, B., & Gates-Williams, J. (1995). Understanding cultural difference in caring for dying patients. *Western Journal of Medicine*, 163(3), 244-249.

23. Brave Heart, M. Y. H., & DeBruyn, L. M. (1998). The American Indian holocaust: Healing historical unresolved grief. *American Indian and Alaska Native Mental Health Research*, 8(2), 56-78.

24. Franklin, A. J. (1999). Invisibility of rage: Racism in psychotherapy with African Americans. In A. J. Franklin (Ed.), *Psychotherapy with African American men* (pp. 17-32). Guilford Press.

25. Helms, J. E., & Cook, D. A. (1999). *Using race and culture in counseling and psychotherapy: Theory and process*. Allyn & Bacon.

26. Pierce, C. M. (1995). Stress analogs of racism and sexism: Terrorism, torture, and disaster. In C. V. Willie, P. P. Rieker, B. M. Kramer, & B. S. Brown (Eds.), *Mental health, racism, and sexism* (pp. 277-293). University of Pittsburgh Press.

27. Constantine, M. G., & Sue, D. W. (2007). Perceptions of racial microaggressions among black supervisees in cross-racial dyads. *Journal of Counseling Psychology*, 54(2), 142-153.

28. Ratts, M. J., Singh, A. A., Nassar-McMillan, S., Butler, S. K., & McCullough, J. R. (2015). Multicultural and social justice counseling competencies. *Journal of Multicultural Counseling and Development*, 44(1), 28-48.

29. Santiago-Rivera, A. L., Arredondo, P., & Gallardo-Cooper, M. (2002). *Counseling Latinos and la familia: A practical guide*. Sage Publications.

30. Organista, K. C. (2007). *Solving Latino psychosocial and health problems: Theory, practice, and populations*. John Wiley & Sons.

31. Cabassa, L. J. (2003). Measuring acculturation: Where we are and where we need to go. *Hispanic Journal of Behavioral Sciences*, 25(2), 127-146.

32. Marin, G., & Marin, B. V. (1991). *Research with Hispanic populations*. Sage Publications.

33. Comas-Díaz, L. (2001). Hispanics, Latinos, or Americanos: The evolution of identity. *Cultural Diversity and Ethnic Minority Psychology*, 7(2), 115-120.

34. Añez, L. M., Paris Jr, M., Bedregal, L. E., Davidson, L., & Grilo, C. M. (2005). Application of cultural constructs in the care of first generation Latino clients in a community mental health setting. *Journal of Psychiatric Practice*, 11(4), 221-230.

35. Interian, A., & Díaz-Martínez, A. M. (2007). Considerations for culturally competent cognitive-behavioral therapy for depression with Hispanic patients. *Cognitive and Behavioral Practice*, 14(1), 84-97.

36. Hernández, M., Nesman, T., Mowery, D., Acevedo-Polakovich, I. D., & Callejas, L. M. (2009). Cultural competence: A literature review and conceptual model for mental health services. *Psychiatric Services*, 60(8), 1046-1050.

37. Grier, W., & Cobbs, P. (1968). *Black rage*. Basic Books.

38. Sue, D. W., Capodilupo, C. M., Torino, G. C., Bucceri, J. M., Holder, A., Nadal, K. L., & Esquilin, M. (2007). Racial

microaggressions in everyday life: Implications for clinical practice. *American Psychologist*, 62(4), 271-286.

39. Boyd-Franklin, N. (2003). *Black families in therapy: Understanding the African American experience* (2nd ed.). Guilford Press.

40. Hines, P. M., & Boyd-Franklin, N. (2005). African American families. In M. McGoldrick, J. Giordano, & N. Garcia-Preto (Eds.), *Ethnicity and family therapy* (3rd ed., pp. 87-100). Guilford Press.

41. Utsey, S. O., Giesbrecht, N., Hook, J., & Stanard, P. M. (2008). Cultural, sociofamilial, and psychological resources that inhibit psychological distress in African Americans exposed to stressful life events and race-related stress. *Journal of Counseling Psychology*, 55(1), 49-62.

42. Snowden, L. R. (2001). Barriers to effective mental health services for African Americans. *Mental Health Services Research*, 3(4), 181-187.

43. Thompson, V. L. S., Bazile, A., & Akbar, M. (2004). African Americans' perceptions of psychotherapy and psychotherapists. *Professional Psychology: Research and Practice*, 35(1), 19-26.

44. Lee, E. (1997). *Working with Asian Americans: A guide for clinicians*. Guilford Press.

45. Uba, L. (1994). *Asian Americans: Personality patterns, identity, and mental health*. Guilford Press.

46. Kim, B. S. K., & Omizo, M. M. (2003). Asian cultural values, attitudes toward seeking professional psychological help, and willingness to see a counselor. *The Counseling Psychologist*, 31(3), 343-361.

47. Zane, N., & Yeh, M. (2002). The use of culturally-based variables in assessment: Studies on loss of face. In K. S.

Kurasaki, S. Okazaki, & S. Sue (Eds.), *Asian American mental health: Assessment theories and methods* (pp. 123-138). Kluwer Academic Publishers.

48. Chung, R. C. Y., & Bemak, F. (2002). The relationship of culture and empathy in cross-cultural counseling. *Journal of Counseling and Development*, 80(2), 154-159.

49. Hong, G. K., & Ham, M. D. (2001). Psychotherapy and counseling with Asian American clients: A practical guide. Sage Publications.

50. Leong, F. T. L., & Lau, A. S. L. (2001). Barriers to providing effective mental health services to Asian Americans. *Mental Health Services Research*, 3(4), 201-214.

51. Root, M. P. P. (1998). Facilitating psychotherapy with Asian American clients. In D. R. Atkinson, G. Morten, & D. W. Sue (Eds.), *Counseling American minorities* (5th ed., pp. 214-234). McGraw-Hill.

52. Sandhu, D. S. (1997). Psychocultural profiles of Asian and Pacific Islander Americans: Implications for counseling and psychotherapy. *Journal of Multicultural Counseling and Development*, 25(1), 7-22.

53. Gone, J. P. (2013). Redressing First Nations historical trauma: Theorizing mechanisms for indigenous culture as mental health treatment. *Transcultural Psychiatry*, 50(5), 683-706.

54. Duran, E., & Duran, B. (1995). *Native American postcolonial psychology*. State University of New York Press.

55. Yellow Horse Brave Heart, M. (2003). The historical trauma response: A pathway to healing. *Journal of Psychoactive Drugs*, 35(1), 7-13.

56. Mohatt, G. V., Thompson, J., Thai, N. D., & Tebes, J. K. (2014). Historical trauma as public narrative: A conceptual

review of how history impacts present-day health. *Social Science & Medicine*, 106, 128-136.

57. Gone, J. P. (2009). A community-based treatment for Native American historical trauma: Prospects for evidence-based practice. *Journal of Consulting and Clinical Psychology*, 77(4), 751-762.

58. Walters, K. L., & Simoni, J. M. (2002). Reconceptualizing native women's health: An "indigenist" stress-coping model. *American Journal of Public Health*, 92(4), 520-524.

59. Whitbeck, L. B., Adams, G. W., Hoyt, D. R., & Chen, X. (2004). Conceptualizing and measuring historical trauma among American Indian people. *American Journal of Community Psychology*, 33(3-4), 119-130.

60. Kading, M. L., Hautala, D., Palombi, L., Aronson, B., Smith, R., & Walls, M. (2015). Flourishing: American Indian positive mental health. *Society and Mental Health*, 5(3), 203-217.

61. BigFoot, D. S., & Schmidt, S. R. (2010). Honoring children, mending the circle: Cultural adaptation of trauma-focused cognitive-behavioral therapy for American Indian and Alaska Native children. *Journal of Clinical Psychology*, 66(8), 847-860.

62. Hodge, D. R. (2005). Social work and the house of Islam: Orienting practitioners to the beliefs and values of Muslims in the United States. *Social Work*, 50(2), 162-173.

63. Al-Krenawi, A., & Graham, J. R. (2000). Culturally sensitive social work practice with Arab clients in mental health settings. *Health & Social Work*, 25(1), 9-22.

64. Amer, M. M., & Hovey, J. D. (2007). Socio-demographic differences in acculturation and mental health for a sample of 2nd generation/early immigrant Arab Americans. *Journal of Immigrant and Minority Health*, 9(4), 335-347.

65. Erickson, C. D., & Al-Timimi, N. R. (2001). Providing mental health services to Arab Americans: Recommendations and considerations. *Cultural Diversity and Ethnic Minority Psychology*, 7(4), 308-327.

66. Jackson, M. L. (1997). Counseling Arab Americans. In C. C. Lee (Ed.), *Multicultural issues in counseling: New approaches to diversity* (2nd ed., pp. 333-349). American Counseling Association.

67. Nassar-McMillan, S. C., & Hakim-Larson, J. (2003). Counseling considerations among Arab Americans. *Journal of Counseling & Development*, 81(2), 150-159.

68. Padela, A. I., & Heisler, M. (2010). The association of perceived abuse and discrimination after September 11, 2001, with psychological distress, level of happiness, and health status among Arab Americans. *American Journal of Public Health*, 100(2), 284-291.

69. Aroian, K. J. (2012). Discrimination against Muslim American adolescents. *Journal of School Nursing*, 28(3), 206-213.

70. Ajrouch, K. J. (2004). Gender, race, and symbolic boundaries: Contested spaces of identity among Arab American adolescents. *Sociological Perspectives*, 47(4), 371-391.

71. Nobles, A. Y., & Sciarra, D. T. (2000). Cultural determinants in the treatment of Arab Americans: A primer for mainstream therapists. *American Journal of Orthopsychiatry*, 70(2), 182-191.

72. Meyer, I. H. (2003). Prejudice, social stress, and mental health in lesbian, gay, and bisexual populations: Conceptual issues and research evidence. *Psychological Bulletin*, 129(5), 674-697.

73. Hendricks, M. L., & Testa, R. J. (2012). A conceptual framework for clinical work with transgender and gender

nonconforming clients: An adaptation of the minority stress model. *Professional Psychology: Research and Practice*, 43(5), 460-467.

74. Pachankis, J. E., & Goldfried, M. R. (2004). Clinical issues in working with lesbian, gay, and bisexual clients. *Psychotherapy: Theory, Research, Practice, Training*, 41(3), 227-246.

75. McCann, E., & Sharek, D. (2014). Challenges to and opportunities for improving mental health services for lesbian, gay, bisexual, and transgender people in Ireland: A narrative account. *International Journal of Mental Health Nursing*, 23(6), 525-533.

76. Balsam, K. F., Martell, C. R., Jones, K. P., & Safren, S. A. (2013). Affirmative cognitive behavior therapy with sexual and gender minority people. In G. Y. Iwamasa & P. A. Hays (Eds.), *Culturally responsive cognitive-behavior therapy: Assessment, practice, and supervision* (pp. 287-314). American Psychological Association.

77. Shelton, K., & Delgado-Romero, E. A. (2011). Sexual orientation microaggressions: The experience of lesbian, gay, bisexual, and queer clients in psychotherapy. *Journal of Counseling Psychology*, 58(2), 210-221.

78. Israel, T., Gorcheva, R., Burnes, T. R., & Walther, W. A. (2008). Helpful and unhelpful therapy experiences of LGBT clients. *Psychotherapy Research*, 18(3), 294-305.

79. Lesbian, Gay, Bisexual, and Transgender Concerns Office, & Committee on Lesbian, Gay, and Bisexual Concerns Joint Task Force. (2000). Guidelines for psychotherapy with lesbian, gay, and bisexual clients. *American Psychologist*, 55(12), 1440-1451.

80. Crisp, C. (2006). The Gay Affirmative Practice Scale (GAP): A new measure for assessing cultural competence with gay and lesbian clients. *Social Work*, 51(2), 115-126.

81. Benson, K. E. (2013). Seeking support: Transgender client experiences with mental health services. *Journal of Feminist Family Therapy*, 25(1), 17-40.

82. Hall, E. T. (1976). *Beyond culture*. Anchor Books.

83. Matsumoto, D., & Hwang, H. S. (2011). Culture and emotion: The integration of biological and cultural contributions. *Journal of Cross-Cultural Psychology*, 42(1), 91-118.

84. Argyle, M. (1988). *Bodily communication* (2nd ed.). Methuen.

85. Ekman, P., & Friesen, W. V. (1969). The repertoire of nonverbal behavior: Categories, origins, usage, and coding. *Semiotica*, 1(1), 49-98.

86. Watson, O. M. (1970). *Proxemic behavior: A cross-cultural study*. Mouton.

87. Shuter, R. (1977). A field study of nonverbal communication in Germany, Italy, and the United States. *Communication Monographs*, 44(4), 298-305.

88. Burgoon, J. K., Buller, D. B., & Woodall, W. G. (1996). *Nonverbal communication: The unspoken dialogue* (2nd ed.). McGraw-Hill.

89. Knapp, M. L., & Hall, J. A. (2010). *Nonverbal communication in human interaction* (7th ed.). Wadsworth.

90. Mehrabian, A. (1971). *Silent messages*. Wadsworth.

91. Tribe, R., & Lane, P. (2009). Working with interpreters across language and culture in mental health. *Journal of Mental Health*, 18(3), 233-241.

92. Flores, G., & Ngui, E. (2006). Racial/ethnic disparities and patient safety. *Pediatric Clinics of North America*, 53(6), 1197-1215.

93. Hsieh, E. (2006). Understanding medical interpreters' role definitions: A psychological perspective. *Patient Education and Counseling*, 62(3), 363-369.

94. Miller, K. E., Martell, Z. L., Pazdirek, L., Caruth, M., & Lopez, D. (2005). The role of interpreters in psychotherapy with refugees: An exploratory study. *American Journal of Orthopsychiatry*, 75(1), 27-39.

95. Searight, H. R., & Armock, J. A. (2013). Foreign language interpreters in mental health: A literature review and research agenda. *North American Journal of Psychology*, 15(1), 17-38.

96. Karliner, L. S., Jacobs, E. A., Chen, A. H., & Mutha, S. (2007). Do professional interpreters improve clinical care for patients with limited English proficiency? A systematic review of the literature. *Health Services Research*, 42(2), 727-754.

97. Bot, H. (2005). *Dialogue interpreting in mental health*. Rodopi.

98. Raval, H., & Smith, J. A. (2003). Therapists' experiences of working with language interpreters. *International Journal of Mental Health*, 32(2), 6-31.

99. Costa, B., & Dewaele, J. M. (2012). Psychotherapy across languages: Beliefs, attitudes and practices of monolingual and multilingual therapists with their multilingual patients. *Language and Psychoanalysis*, 1(1), 18-40.

100. D'Ardenne, P., Ruaro, L., Cestari, L., Fakhoury, W., & Priebe, S. (2007). Does interpreter-mediated CBT with traumatized refugee people work? A comparison of patient outcomes in East London. *Behavioural and Cognitive Psychotherapy*, 35(3), 293-301.

101. Ho, M. K. (1987). *Family therapy with ethnic minorities*. Sage Publications.

102.   Minuchin, S., & Fishman, H. C. (1981). *Family therapy techniques*. Harvard University Press.

103.   Aponte, H. J., & VanDeusen, J. M. (1981). Structural family therapy. In A. S. Gurman & D. P. Kniskern (Eds.), *Handbook of family therapy* (pp. 310-360). Brunner/Mazel.

104.   Szapocznik, J., & Kurtines, W. M. (1989). *Breakthroughs in family therapy with drug-abusing and problem youth*. Springer.

105.   La Roche, M. J., & Maxie, A. (2003). Ten considerations in addressing cultural differences in psychotherapy. *Professional Psychology: Research and Practice*, 34(2), 180-186.

106.   Pargament, K. I. (2007). *Spiritually integrated psychotherapy: Understanding and addressing the sacred*. Guilford Press.

107.   Miller, W. R. (1999). *Integrating spirituality into treatment: Resources for practitioners*. American Psychological Association.

108.   Richards, P. S., & Bergin, A. E. (2005). *A spiritual strategy for counseling and psychotherapy* (2nd ed.). American Psychological Association.

109.   Sperry, L. (2012). *Spirituality in clinical practice: Theory and practice of spiritually oriented psychotherapy* (2nd ed.). Routledge.

110.   Pargament, K. I., Koenig, H. G., & Perez, L. M. (2000). The many methods of religious coping: Development and initial validation of the RCOPE. *Journal of Clinical Psychology*, 56(4), 519-543.

111.   Hodge, D. R. (2006). A template for spiritual assessment: A review of the JCAHO requirements and guidelines for implementation. *Social Work*, 51(4), 317-326.

112.   Koenig, H. G. (2012). Religion, spirituality, and mental health: A review and meta-analysis. *Journal of Health Psychology*, 17(6), 725-735.

113.   Frame, M. W. (2003). *Integrating religion and spirituality into counseling: A comprehensive approach.* Brooks/Cole.

114.   Cashwell, C. S., & Young, J. S. (2011). *Integrating spirituality and religion into counseling: A guide to competent practice* (2nd ed.). American Counseling Association.

115.   Post, B. C., & Wade, N. G. (2009). Religion and spirituality in psychotherapy: A practice-friendly review of research. *Journal of Clinical Psychology*, 65(2), 131-146.

116.   Cross, T., Bazron, B., Dennis, K., & Isaacs, M. (1989). *Towards a culturally competent system of care.* Georgetown University Child Development Center.

117.   Betancourt, J. R., Green, A. R., Carrillo, J. E., & Ananeh-Firempong, O. (2003). Defining cultural competence: A practical framework for addressing racial/ethnic disparities in health and health care. *Public Health Reports*, 118(4), 293-302.

118.   Brach, C., & Fraser, I. (2000). Can cultural competency reduce racial and ethnic health disparities? A review and conceptual model. *Medical Care Research and Review*, 57(1), 181-217.

119.   Miranda, J., Bernal, G., Lau, A., Kohn, L., Hwang, W. C., & LaFromboise, T. (2005). State of the science on psychosocial interventions for ethnic minorities. *Annual Review of Clinical Psychology*, 1, 113-142.

120.   Alegría, M., Vallas, M., & Pumariega, A. J. (2010). Racial and ethnic disparities in pediatric mental health. *Child and Adolescent Psychiatric Clinics of North America*, 19(4), 759-774.

121.   Substance Abuse and Mental Health Services Administration. (2014). *Improving cultural competence.* Treatment Improvement Protocol (TIP) Series 59. SAMHSA.

122.   Benish, S. G., Quintana, S., & Wampold, B. E. (2011). Culturally adapted psychotherapy and the legitimacy of myth: A direct-comparison meta-analysis. *Journal of Counseling Psychology*, 58(3), 279-289.

123.   Smith, T. B., Rodríguez, M. D., & Bernal, G. (2011). Culture. *Journal of Clinical Psychology*, 67(2), 166-175.

124.   Griner, D., & Smith, T. B. (2006). Culturally adapted mental health intervention: A meta-analytic review. *Psychotherapy: Theory, Research, Practice, Training*, 43(4), 531-548.

125.   La Roche, M. J., & Christopher, M. S. (2009). Changing paradigms from empirically supported treatment to evidence-based practice: A cultural perspective. *Professional Psychology: Research and Practice*, 40(4), 396-402.

www.ingramcontent.com/pod-product-compliance
Lightning Source LLC
Chambersburg PA
CBHW062220270326
41930CB00009B/1809